"In *Exploring the Paranormal* Christian scholar R. Alan Streett recounts his half-century-long journey into the captivating world of paranormal experiences — spiritual healings, clairvoyance, spirit contact, magic, and beyond — meeting the fascinating practitioners and encountering the intellectual challenges of mapping the subconscious world where mind, psyche, and spirit converge and interact. And he does this all while trying to develop a mature Christian commitment and remain true to an orthodox theological heritage. Readers will be caught up in the unexpected twists and turns as new encounters force thoughtful changes upon the seeker-pilgrim."

—J. GORDON MELTON
Baylor University

"In *Exploring the Paranormal*, Alan Streett takes us on a journey to the edge of the spiritual frontiers and explains how faith, when triggered in the brain by an unexpected word, event, sight, thought, or even a serendipitous encounter, can produce amazing results, including physical healing and spiritual breakthroughs. Broadly speaking, faith is our sixth sense that unlocks the mysteries of the world around us. It views as real what the five natural senses cannot comprehend. In this book, theology and psychology meet at the intersection of the spirit and mind."

—HAROLD G. KOENIG
director of the Center for Spirituality, Theology and Health
Duke University

"Alan Streett takes us on an astonishing journey. This is a memoir of sorts, tracing Streett's life from accomplished baseball player to theology professor, though one centered on the author's longtime engagement with and study of spiritualism, psychic phenomena, and all things paranormal. In a world increasingly at home with 'spiritual, not religious,' this book is a fascinating read."

—JOEL B. GREEN
Fuller Theological Seminary

T0314581

"Alan Streett conveys the most powerful and precious insight: that the presence of the sacred is real and surrounds us. Here and now, we all have the opportunity to seek, to open our spiritual awareness, to awaken [to its existence]."

—LISA MILLER
founder of the Spirituality Mind Body Institute at
Columbia University

"Alan Streett has spent a lifetime seeking to understand the nature of the paranormal. Dissatisfied with typical evangelical explanations, he follows the trail of evidence wherever it leads and invites us to join him. Along the way we encounter psychic healers, trance mediums, Christian mystics, and even a few hucksters — all claiming to have transcendental experiences. As he separates fact from fantasy, Streett draws surprising conclusions about these extraordinary occurrences. *Exploring the Paranormal* is a real page turner!"

—JONATHAN MERRITT
contributor to *The Atlantic* and
columnist for Religion News Service

EXPLORING THE
PARANORMAL

Miracles, Magic, and the Mysterious

R. ALAN STREETT

WILLIAM B. EERDMANS PUBLISHING COMPANY
GRAND RAPIDS, MICHIGAN

Wm. B. Eerdmans Publishing Co.
4035 Park East Court SE, Grand Rapids, Michigan 49546
www.eerdmans.com

Book design by Lydia Hall

Printed in the United States of America

30 29 28 27 26 25 24   1 2 3 4 5 6 7

ISBN 978-0-8028-8453-4

Library of Congress Cataloging-in-Publication Data

A catalog record for this book is available from
the Library of Congress.

Dedicated to the memory of William Theodore (Ted) Swager

Friend, fellow minister, and seeker of truth

CONTENTS

FOREWORD

Most of the time when academics write books, we share our conclusions. We make arguments for those conclusions, of course, but we reveal little about the process that led us to them. That is certainly what I generally do, and to be clear, I am not in any way denigrating the value and importance of our scholarly publications of that more typical sort. However, it is much rarer, and much too infrequent, to have a chance to hear an account of someone's intellectual journey, the path of discovery that led them from wherever they started, through various twists and turns, to new insights and understanding different from what they had before. To get an account of that journey, we usually have to know the individual in question and be treated to a brief summary of their process. If an academic writes a memoir (there isn't much of a market for those even from the most famous scholars) the story aims to be more comprehensive, encompassing the life and career as a whole. Thus what Al Streett has provided readers with here in *Exploring the Paranormal: Miracles, Magic, and the Mysterious* is something that is both extremely rare and extremely valuable. He takes us on a journey lasting many years, allows us to see the world as he once saw it, and leads us step by step to explore and to change our minds along with him. He does so on a topic that divides Christians from one another and that fascinates most of us, yet which few of us investigate through experience and research in anything that comes close to the extent that Al has. We would be privileged if he had shared just the results of his lifelong investigation in the more usual fashion. What he has offered us is much richer, more readable, and more potentially life-transforming.

My own journey of interest in the paranormal and supernatural is much less interesting than Al's, but there were enough parallels that I could relate to his interests every step of the way and fill in gaps or answer unresolved questions that had been part of my own exploration. I am certain this will be true for many readers, whose curiosity and eagerness to understand and experience are mirrored in Al's own, and yet who never researched the various aspects of the topic in such a thorough way. Growing up, I had both a religious upbringing and a love of fantasy literature. Both led me to expect the world to be a place full of magic and mysteries. I also had a deep love for and interest in science. At least when we are young, those two loves do not seem incompatible in the way that they tend to in our later years, and that bifurcation is precisely one of the crucially important topics that is addressed by the end of Al's journey. In ages past, all of it was an attempt to understand and, to the extent possible, harness the power latent in a world whose character and possibilities we have even now only begun to fathom. That is why so many of the pioneering scientists and explorers of the natural world were also explorers of the mind and of things esoteric, and why the literary boundaries between science fiction and fantasy are so porous and permeable, as too are those between scientific and spiritual interest in UFOs.

In my teens, when I had a born-again experience in a Pentecostal church, I redefined the magical as the occult, something demonic, and replaced interest in the *paranormal* with a desire to experience more and more of the *supernatural*. Eventually two things combined to shift my interest away from a faith focused on experience. One was study of both the Bible and science; the other was encountering religious people from other traditions who described having spiritual experiences that resembled my own. The initial instinct is to insist that such things are demonic deceptions. After all, how could one believe such radically different doctrines and yet have a genuine experience of God? That of course leaves one with a serious conundrum: how can I be sure that I'm not the one deceived rather than them? There's nothing like that paradox to shift one's focus away from experience onto theology and doctrine. Yet at the foundation of my personal faith was still that experience that had changed my life and set me on a path that I am continuing to travel today. Initially I shielded my born-again experience from scrutiny. It wasn't psychological, I insisted, but *spiritual*. Eventually I realized that my antithesis was a false one. Experiences, and our memories of them, cannot be separated from the mind, from the brain. For a long time, as someone who had bought briefly into pseudoscience that I thought was inseparable from my faith, and who had replaced a youthful eagerness to believe and to feel with a more skeptical demeanor, I didn't know what to do with all this, and I shied away from giving the matter too much attention.

Then along came Al's book. I started reading the prepublication manuscript on a trip, taking along a few things to read, but those other books didn't get much attention. Once I started reading Al's book, I couldn't stop. I had expected it to be about mind, miracles, and magic, and it is, but I did not expect him to narrate his own personal experiences, his journey. I have valued his academic books in the past, and it turns out he's skilled at writing memoir too. But this is no ordinary memoir. This is the academic and spiritual equivalent of the memoir of your favorite musician, who tells you their life's story with a focus on the music. It is a book that I am sure will be inspirational both for your spirituality and for your intellect, both coming together in the life of the mind. As Al's book came to a close I found it had encouraged me to view my own exploration as not yet done. I hope that as you join him on this journey it will not only help you resolve things you may have wrestled with or wondered about in the past but will convince you that there's more to learn and explore.

One last thing. Read the footnotes. Seriously, I can't believe that statements as profound as this — "I discovered that the key to having a relationship with God did not come by repeating a formulaic prayer but by surrendering one's will to God" — are relegated to footnotes. I share it here so you don't miss it and because it will help you appreciate my enthusiasm for the book you're about to read. If the footnotes are this rich, imagine what lies in store for you in the main text!

JAMES F. MCGRATH
Clarence L. Goodwin Chair in
New Testament Language and Literature,
Butler University

PART 1

I

My Quest

Spoken words are powerful. I should know. When I was eleven years old and playing Little League, a stranger came up after a game and said, "Young man, keep working hard, and one day I'll sign you to a Major League contract." Handing me his business card, he patted me on the shoulder and departed. I glanced down to read: *Joe Consoli, Regional Scout, Pittsburgh Pirates Baseball Club*. My heart skipped a beat, and I rushed to tell my dad what had just happened.

To my knowledge, Joe Consoli never knew the impact of his words. But from that day forward, I dreamed of playing professional baseball.

Top-notch amateur catchers are hard to find. Very few can read a batter, control the pitcher, call a good game, block balls in the dirt to the right and left, throw out base runners, catch pop flies, and endure the physical abuse of balls pounding their body from head to toe. I cannot count the number of times foul tips struck my face mask with such force that I could smell chemicals being released from my brain. I didn't learn until much later in life that baseball aficionados jokingly refer to catchers' gear as "the tools of ignorance." Had I known, I likely would have chosen a different position.

Over the next several years, baseball was my life. I had no girlfriend, didn't attend Saturday night dances, or hang out at local burger joints like others. Instead, I played baseball five nights a week and doubleheaders on Sundays on some of the best teams on the East Coast.[1] Their rosters were filled with like-minded kids whose only goal was to make it to the majors.[2] We were all top-notch players, but I had an added incentive — Joe Consoli's words.

I entered the University of Baltimore in fall 1964. The following spring, I won the starting catcher's spot and an athletic scholarship. I excelled both in the field and at bat, and ran the sixty-yard dash in 6.9 seconds, which for a catcher was quite speedy. The "Bees," as we were known, played in the Mason Dixon Conference. In my junior year (1967) we captured the league championship and competed for the small-college (NCAA, Division II) championship in Springfield, Massachusetts.

Major League scouts from several teams showed up at most of my games. And I thought I had a good chance of signing with one of them. Joe Consoli had recently told me I had a *Major League arm* and

1. In the summer of 1963, I won the starting spot as catcher for G&M Scrap, the premier fourteen-to-sixteen-year-old team in the greater Baltimore area. The coach, Sterling "Sheriff" Fowble, a former minor league player, was a legend in amateur baseball circles. He demanded excellence from his players and got it, and led his team to eight consecutive Baltimore city championships. The dark green cap with the gold *G* logo identified you as one of the "Sheriff's Boys." Incidentally, when I tried out for my high school JV team the year before, I was cut after the first week of practice. The following year, however, when I walked onto the high school field wearing my G&M cap, the varsity head coach treated me like royalty and said I would be a key player in his starting lineup. Still chafing from being cut from JV the year before, I walked into the coach's office, quit the team, turned in my uniform, and never looked back. It was sweet revenge at the time. In hindsight, I now believe I made a rash decision. It would have been nice to play for my high school team.

2. Many of my teammates signed professional contracts to play baseball, some made it to the Major Leagues, and at least two were elected to the Baseball Hall of Fame in Cooperstown, New York.

compared it to that of Elston Howard, the New York Yankees all-star catcher. My head swelled.

THE INJURY

At the beginning of my senior year, the unimaginable happened! On a frigid afternoon in February 1968, while taking infield practice, something snapped in my right shoulder. A sharp pain shot down the length of my arm. I knew intuitively it was a severe injury. My arm went limp, and when I lifted it to throw another ball, the pain increased. My arm throbbed.

The school trainer packed my shoulder in ice and ordered me into the whirlpool. Nothing helped. As soon as I got back on the field and threw the ball, it was like someone had stabbed me with a hunting knife. If I didn't get help soon, I would be sitting on the bench for the opening game.

I sought medical help from my family doctor, who gave me a shot of cortisone and suggested two more treatments. The treatments failed to alleviate the problem. In desperation, I visited an orthopedist, who suggested exploratory surgery. In a day when MRIs were nonexistent, surgery was the only means to determine the nature and extent of my problem.

Gripped by an irrational fear of dying on the operating table, I sought an alternative solution. I stopped by the Pimlico Racetrack and bought a bottle of strong horse liniment. If it worked for thoroughbreds, it might work for me![3] The concoction succeeded only in removing a few layers of my skin, but not the pain.

On opening day, the coach moved me to first base. The scouts soon discovered why, and I felt my chances of signing a pro contract quickly slipping away.

3. I lived only three blocks from the Pimlico Racetrack, the home of the Preakness Stakes.

In an act of desperation, I did the unthinkable. I visited a psychic healer!

OLGA WORRALL

Olga Worrall was an internationally famous and well-respected psychic healer who lived in Baltimore and held weekly healing services at a local church. She claimed that highly sensitive cameras were able to capture on celluloid streams of energy emanating from her fingertips.[4]

I first learned of Olga when my mother handed me a copy of Olga's autobiography, *The Gift of Healing*.[5] She had just finished reading it and said, "Maybe you should go see Olga." At first, I scoffed at the suggestion but then reasoned, *What do I have to lose?* I picked up the book and started to read the amazing story.

Olga Nathalie Ripich was born November 30, 1906, in Cleveland, Ohio, to Russian immigrants. Her father was a theology professor in the Russian Orthodox Church. At an early age Olga said she saw and spoke with the spirits of dead relatives who visited her at night. In a letter she wrote to me some years later, she said, "My parents became aware of my gifts when I was only eight years old . . . and praised God for [them]." As word spread of the youngster's visions, neighbors sought her out for a spiritual blessing or healing touch. Her prayers were most effective when she placed her hands on the temples of those suffering from migraine headaches.

In 1927 Olga met Ambrose Alexander Worrall, a mechanical engineer for the Martin Aircraft Corporation in Baltimore, whom she married the following year. He, too, was a mystic of sorts and con-

---

4. This photographic technique is known as Kirlian photography. Developed in the 1960s, it purportedly captured the images of the aura or energy field that surrounded the human body.

5. Olga Worrall and Ambrose Worrall, *The Gift of Healing* (New York: Harper & Row, 1965).

fessed to seeing auras, that is, energy fields engulfing the human body. He believed one's health was linked to the color of one's aura. A blue-colored aura signified good health, green pointed to sickness, black to imminent death, and so forth. Ambrose approached psychic phenomena from a scientific angle while Olga looked at them from a spiritual point of view. They made a good team. Together they wrote articles and books, lectured at professional psychic conferences, and were interviewed on radio and television. Of the two, Olga was the best known, mainly because of her healing powers.

My own family was no stranger to the world of the occult. My father had an uncanny and mysterious ability to remove warts. People often sought him out. He took them aside and talked quietly with them for a few minutes. A week or two later the warts were gone! I later asked him how he accomplished this. "If I tell you," he said, "I will lose my ability." He did mention that years before, a man whom he did not identify transferred to him this special power. In turn, my father was allowed to share the secret with only one other person in his lifetime, which he said he had already done. When I questioned my mother, she thought my father performed some ritual or uttered a secret prayer.

My mother also told me that my uncle John was able to remove pain from burn victims and that local fire departments often called on him at all hours of the day or night. Known as "drawing out fire," the ritual involved waving hands above the burns and mumbling magical words. This undisclosed technique was passed down orally from generation to generation to ensure that the practice never died out.

The New Life Clinic

As I finished reading Olga's story, I decided to seek her help. Mount Washington United Methodist Church, a small white frame structure, was over a century old and located in a rustic section of Baltimore County. The building now sits in a valley beneath the Jones Falls Expressway, where thousands of cars pass overhead every day without knowing a church sits below. Yet for two decades people from across America came to Baltimore to attend the New Life Clinic, the official name of Olga's weekly healing ministry.

I headed across town to join others seeking relief from various ailments ranging from brain tumors to aches and pains. Arriving forty-five minutes early, I was surprised to find the parking lot already filled. I ended up parking on the street two blocks away. As I entered the building, I saw a sign pointing to a set of stairs — one to the left and the other to the right — that led up to the second-floor sanctuary. The auditorium overflowed with people — some in wheelchairs lining the aisles, a few bald-headed children wearing bandannas cuddled next to a parent, and others bent over in pain or with limbs in plaster casts, but most showed no visible signs of illness. I spotted an empty seat in the back row. Squeezing past several people, I sat down and waited anxiously.

At 10 a.m. sharp, a short gray-headed lady in her sixties entered the auditorium by a side door near the pulpit. *That's Olga?* She looked more like a kindly grandmother than a psychic healer. Two men followed, who I later learned were Rev. Robert Kirkley, the church's pastor, and a trusted church lay leader. All wore black clergy robes and stood behind the altar rail facing the audience.

"Welcome to the New Life Clinic," Olga gently intoned. "You are here today because you have need for physical healing." She added confidently, "God's healing power is available to all regardless of religious affiliation." That was music to my ears, since I had rarely darkened the door of a church building.

Then in a sterner voice, she declared, "I am not a *faith* healer. But my hands are channels of healing energy. It's all scientific." Olga ended her remarks by reminding us that she never charges for her services.

Olga then invited those seeking healing to move to the aisle and come to the front. Lines formed immediately in front of the three intercessors. As an organ played softly, I contemplated the right moment to approach Olga. Timing was everything. I didn't want to find myself standing before one of her assistants. I was extremely cautious and finally made my move and headed straight for Olga, knelt at the altar rail, and briefly told her about my injury. She listened patiently and intently before placing her hands on my face and praying silently. *Is that it?* I thought. *Why don't I feel any energy flowing from her hands?* Olga must have sensed my disappointment because she clutched my wrists as I got up to leave and said, "When the meeting is over, I would like to speak with you." She then patted my hand, and I returned to my seat. I didn't know what to make of the meeting. It was not what I expected. The low-key service was devoid of all emotion. No one raised their hands or shouted, "Hallelujah!" I witnessed no spectacular healings. No one preached a sermon or took up an offering.

Prior to his closing benediction, Rev. Kirkley announced that a light lunch would be served at minimal cost in the fellowship hall on the first level. He invited all to stay. The three ministers left just as they had arrived — through a rear door behind the pulpit. The people slowly filed out, but I stayed behind. Just when I thought Olga had forgotten me, she suddenly appeared and said with a smile, "Let's have lunch. You must tell me all about yourself."

LUNCH WITH OLGA

Olga and I sat at a head table, along with a few other guests and visiting ministers. She asked about my hopes, dreams, and plans. But mainly she wanted to introduce me to the *who*, *what*, and *where* of the world of parapsychology.[6] It was like taking a crash course in PSI 101 taught by a great master. We were engrossed in conversation when a tall, thin man with salt-and-pepper hair and sunken cheeks tapped his fork on a water glass. He rose to make a few announcements. "The next Spiritual Frontiers Fellowship meeting will meet at the Grace United Methodist Church." Olga leaned closer and explained, "Spiritual Frontiers is a group that seeks to introduce psychic gifts into the mainline churches. You should attend."

---

6. Parapsychology goes by different names, including ESP, PSI, occultism, psychic phenomena, etc. See the glossary.

Then the lanky announcer, who bore a striking resemblance to Michael Rennie, the star of the cult classic *The Day the Earth Stood Still*,[7] invited us to browse the book table before we departed. With that, Olga excused herself momentarily and soon returned with a packet of papers.

"Here is a list of the best books on parapsychology. Start reading," she instructed. "Begin with *There Is a River*, the story of Edgar Cayce. You'll love it."

As we said our good-byes, Olga encouraged me to make an appointment with a Dr. Richard Adolph, the chiropractor for the Baltimore Colts football team.

"He is the best in the business, and he is one of us," she said as she reached out her hand and wished me well.

On my drive home, my mind raced a mile a minute: *Why would a renowned psychic healer recommend I visit a chiropractor? After all, wasn't she the one with healing hands?*

Nonetheless, I followed Olga's orders. I made an appointment with Dr. Adolph, who said, "Don't worry, pal, I'll fix you up," but after several visits I felt no relief.

7. The 1951 original, not the 2008 remake.

2

SPIRITUAL FRONTIERS
FELLOWSHIP

G etting on the parapsychology bandwagon is like taking your first
ride on a roller coaster. It is both scary and exhilarating at the
same time. Each month, the Baltimore chapter of the Spiritual Frontiers Fellowship (SFF) met in the beautiful sanctuary of the Grace United Methodist Church, one of the largest and most prestigious churches in the
city. Located in a well-to-do neighborhood, the church boasted members who were the crème de la crème of society. Many respected clergy,
including John Wesley Lord, bishop of the Baltimore-Washington
Conference of the United Methodist Church, were advocates of psychic exploration and attended SFF gatherings regularly.[1]

On a brisk night in March, I joined about two hundred others who
were in search of the supernatural. I was somewhat apprehensive since
I didn't know what to expect. At seven o'clock, a short, rotund man

---

1. John Wesley Lord, for example, later wrote the back-cover endorsement
for Ambrose Worrall and Olga Worrall, *Explore Your Psychic World* (New York:
Harper & Row, 1970).

with a kindly smile ascended the podium and welcomed us. He introduced himself as Ambrose Worrall.

What a surprise!

I didn't expect to meet Ambrose. After a few introductory remarks, he offered his perspective on the paranormal: "All psychic phenomena have a rational explanation and a scientific foundation. What we call supernatural experiences, in fact, are quite natural. We simply haven't discovered the laws that govern them. Our knowledge is quite limited."

With a bit of excitement in his voice, Ambrose introduced the speaker for the evening — Cleve Backster, a polygraph expert from New York, who had conducted some eye-opening experiments with plants.

Backster, sporting a flattop, was a down-to-earth, no-nonsense kind of guy who owned a polygraph school in New York City. Respected in his field, he was often sought out by the New York Police Department to assist in solving crimes. In his hour-long presentation he recalled his happenstance discovery of the conscious awareness of plant life.

On a lark, Backster attached a sensitive polygraph electrode to the leaf of a potted plant in his living room. To his surprise, the polygraph needle recorded a response. *How odd*, he thought. *Plants don't possess consciousness.*

With the clip still attached, he tore off another leaf from the same plant. The original leaf immediately reacted. Caught off guard, Backster talked out loud to himself: "Is it possible that one leaf of a plant feels pain when another is injured?"

He next plucked off a leaf from a different plant that sat across the room. The results were the same. Distance did not matter! With his curiosity pricked, he wondered if the original leaf might react if harm comes to another life-form. At the opposite end of the house, he filled a fish tank with scalding water and dropped in a dozen brine shrimp. The leaf in the other room responded violently.

Backster's presentation was timely since "talking to your plants" was in vogue. It was a topic of conversation at cocktail parties and dinner tables. Daytime TV talk-show hosts discussed it and stand-up comedians joked about it. But Backster wasn't kidding. He concluded his talk and slideshow with a challenge to treat all life with reverence because it possesses a level of conscious existence.

At the end of the evening, Ambrose Worrall announced the date of the next meeting and also invited us to hang around for light refreshments. Before I departed, I picked up several brochures describing the origin, nature, and mission of the SFF.

History of the SFF

The SFF, founded on March 5, 1956, in Chicago, was the brainchild of three prominent clergymen: Paul Higgins, a Methodist pastor; Albin Bro, PhD, a former missionary and educator; and Arthur Ford, a Disciples of Christ minister and well-known trance medium. They wished to reawaken mainline churches to the supernatural reality as found in the pages of the Bible. When first-century Jesus followers gathered, God's Spirit moved and they witnessed and received healings, prophecies, Spirit-induced revelations, visons, and dreams. According to the SFF, they fell into trances (Acts 22:17), saw things from afar (John 1:48), were mysteriously transported (Acts 8:39), encountered angels (Luke 2:8–20), and occasionally spoke with the dead (Matt. 17:3). Over the centuries, the churches unfortunately lost touch with the supernatural. The SFF hoped to guide the church back to its spiritual roots.[2]

The organizational meeting of the SFF, held at Hyde Street Methodist Church in Chicago, was by invitation only. One hundred participants, mainly ministers and lay leaders associated with a variety of denominations (Baptist, Presbyterian, Quaker, Methodist, Congregational, Lutheran, and Dutch Reformed, among others), attended from all parts of the United States. They sang, prayed, shared meals, and

---

2. For a detailed account of SFF's founding and expansion, see William V. Rauscher, *The Spiritual Frontier* (New York: Doubleday, 1975).

discussed the need for an organization like SFF. On the last evening Arthur Ford conducted a trance session in which disembodied spirits of the dead spoke through his vocal cords. Ford believed that spiritualism offered proof that the soul survives death.

Ford's séance caused quite a stir. Some attendees viewed it as the spiritual highlight of the conference while others expressed grave concern. Nevertheless, all agreed that trances and communication with the "other side" had biblical support. After all, Jesus spoke with Moses and Elijah on the Mount of Transfiguration as Peter, James, and John looked on (Matt. 17:1–8).

At the conclusion of the meetings, the majority of participants voted to start psychic study groups under the auspices of SFF in their respective churches and dioceses. They also elected a board of directors consisting of ministers and respected businesspeople, all of whom affirmed traditional Christian beliefs as expressed in the Apostles' and Nicene Creeds. In time, SFF grew exponentially until it sponsored chapters in all fifty states and the District of Columbia with a dues-paying membership that exceeded ten thousand.

✦

I attended several more SFF meetings and searched for the books on Olga's reading list. The Aquarian Age Bookstore, an obscure second-floor shop on North Charles Street that specialized in esoterica, had the best selection. The first time I visited, my senses were bombarded by smells of incense, sounds of New Age music, and the vivid colors of psychedelic posters hanging from the walls. The salesclerk, wearing a ponytail, sandals, and a pair of John Lennon glasses, gave me the once over. Dressed in a button-down shirt, khaki slacks, and a pair of Jack Purcells, I was not his typical customer.

The store carried hundreds of titles dealing with UFOs, reincarnation, talking to the dead, angels, meditation, and the lives of yogis. I knew I had stumbled onto the mother lode. It was hard to choose one book, so I settled on *There Is a River*, which was at the top of Olga's recommended reading list.[3] Written by journalist Thomas Sugrue, this fascinating biography of Edgar Cayce, "the Sleeping Prophet," read like a novel. I couldn't put it down. As a result, I bought every book I could find on Cayce.

Edgar Cayce (1877–1945) was best known for his ability to diagnose illnesses and prescribe medical treatments while in a trance. He discovered this unique ability after developing a chronic case of laryngitis. Despite numerous visits to the doctor, his condition worsened. In desperation, he turned to a traveling hypnotist, who restored Cayce's voice. It seemed like a miracle, but within days the hoarseness returned.

Hoping for a permanent remedy, Cayce tried self-hypnosis. He discovered that during a trance he was able to diagnose the cause of his problem and find the solution. Word soon got out about Cayce's miracle cure. Others sought his help. Over the next decade, Cayce, a professional photographer by trade, took daily breaks at 10 a.m. and 2 p.m., hypnotized himself, analyzed people who visited his studio, and proposed treatments for them. Many claimed healing. While entranced, Cayce often used long medical terms he could not pronounce or understand while awake.

People from far away wrote letters and sent telegraphs requesting Cayce's help. He soon learned that distance was no factor. As he reclined on his couch and fell into a sleep-like state, he could see the people and discern their problems. His secretary sat next to him and took verbatim notes, which were mailed to the inquirers, with duplicates being placed in files.

As the files grew, they were compiled and indexed according to ailments, diagnoses, and treatments. Over time, they were edited and transformed into a three-hundred-page volume called the "black book."

3. Thomas Sugrue, *There Is a River: The Story of Edgar Cayce* (New York: Dell, 1967).

As Cayce's reputation spread, the *New York Times* ran a story with the bold headline "ILLITERATE MAN BECOMES A DOCTOR WHEN HYPNOTIZED."[4] Overnight, requests from around the nation flooded his mailbox. For the next decade, Cayce continued to offer free consultations, believing his paranormal powers came from God.

In 1923, Art Lammers, a wealthy printer from Dayton, Ohio, and a proponent of Theosophy, visited Cayce and made a strange request. He did not seek medical help but wanted Cayce (while in trance) to answer a series of questions about esoteric subjects. Cayce gave it a try. Lammers asked about reincarnation, karma, and the lost continent of Atlantis, among other matters. This was the start of Cayce's metaphysical or "life readings."

When Cayce later read the transcription of the session, he was shocked. His answers conflicted with his own beliefs as a lifelong Christian and Sunday school teacher. Had he contacted a demonic source? Lammers persuaded him otherwise. In the end, Cayce theorized he had somehow tapped into a cumulative reservoir of human knowledge — dubbed the "Akashic records" — stored on the ethereal plane.

Cayce continued to give both medical and life readings, over fourteen thousand in all.

In 1925, Morton Blumenthal, a wealthy New York businessman, offered Cayce the financial wherewithal to devote full-time attention to his readings. When the millionaire learned that Cayce dreamed of building a hospital where physicians could treat their patients based on his trance diagnoses, Blumenthal offered to fund the entire project. Several readings identified Virginia Beach as the ideal location. By 1928, a fully equipped hospital was up and running. Two years later, Cayce opened Atlantic University, where students could earn a liberal arts degree and study holistic principles. Dr. William Brown, a distinguished professor at Washington and Lee University, served as its first president. The freshman class exceeded two hundred students. Cayce was on top of the world. Then the stock market crash of 1929

4. *New York Times*, October 9, 1910.

wiped out Blumenthal's fortune. Both the hospital and school closed their doors, the Virginia Beach property was sold, and all employees were laid off.

To survive, Cayce formed the nonprofit Association for Research and Enlightenment (ARE) and solicited financial support from family and friends. The response was overwhelming and enabled Cayce to give free readings until his death in 1945.

Several best-selling biographies were published after Cayce's passing that increased his popularity and mystique. A movement grew up around the "Sleeping Prophet," and many people for the first time learned about his miracle cures and esoteric teachings. Under the visionary leadership of his eldest son, Hugh Lynn Cayce, the ARE membership exploded. In 1956, the ARE repurchased the land and original hospital building. The beautifully landscaped property and modernized facilities now serve as the group's headquarters.

After reading *There Is a River*, I became an ARE member. Benefits included a subscription to the bimonthly magazine, a copy of the "black book," free admission to all lectures at the headquarters, and access to the library that housed Cayce's archives.

My Senior Year Comes to an End

I had recently changed my major from history to psychology in accordance with my new interests. Dr. Raymond Nell, the head of the department, believed humans possessed many senses beyond recognized taste, smell, hearing, touch, and sight, and prompted his students to explore psychic phenomena. Dr. Ralph Funkhouser, however, was my favorite professor. I looked forward to taking all of his classes. So, my heart sank when he announced at the last class of his "Abnormal Psychology" course that he was leaving the University of Baltimore to take a position as an administrator of a state-run psychiatric facility.

Before wishing us a final good-bye, he said he wanted to leave us with a piece of advice. We all sat up in anticipation. Dr. Funkhouser said that, from a psychological standpoint, guilt is the underlying cause of most psychological problems. The only remedy for guilt is forgiveness. Dr. Funkhouser then unexpectedly spoke of the importance of Jesus Christ and how his death on the cross is the source of all forgiveness. Jesus's last words on earth were, "Father, forgive them." Funkhouser ended his short talk by challenging us to find forgiveness through Jesus Christ. By inviting Christ into our hearts, he said, we could find freedom from sin and guilt. He then wished us a farewell and a good summer.

The whole episode was surreal and somewhat embarrassing. I looked around and saw several students squirming uncomfortably in their seats. I was one of them!

As students said good-bye to each other until next semester and filed out of the classroom, many awkwardly walked past Dr. Funkhouser and avoided eye contact. Despite the discomfort of the moment, I stayed back long enough to thank him for the impact he had on my college life. A tear came to his eye.

Driving home, I contemplated Funkhouser's remarks and replayed the scene over in my mind.

I never considered myself a religious person, although I prayed whenever I needed a base hit or faced a difficult personal problem. Later that night, as I lay in bed, exhausted and emotionally drained, I fell asleep uttering a short prayer: *Christ, I am a sinner. Come into my life and forgive me.* The next morning, when I awoke, nothing had changed. I didn't feel forgiven or reconciled to God.

Was something wrong with me? Or was Funkhouser some sort of religious fanatic?

I had a difficult time processing it all; so, to be safe, I repeated that same prayer for forgiveness every night for the next three years. There was no noticeable change.

Hope Renewed

I ended my senior season at first base with the highest batting average of my college career, but my arm was no better. When the Major League draft was held in June, no team offered me a contract.

Frank Sansosti, a regional scout for the Cleveland Indians, suggested I consider playing ball in the Shenandoah Valley League, consisting of twelve semipro teams located along the Blue Ridge Mountains of Virginia. Top undrafted East Coast juniors and seniors in college filled their rosters. Sansosti said many scouts patrolled the summer league for prospects, and if I could somehow work out my arm problems, I might draw their attention. With a few phone calls, he arranged for me to report to the Craigsville Cardinals.

Before heading toward the Valley, I made an appointment with my family physician to see, if by chance, he had another idea on how to relieve the constant pain in my right shoulder. He told me of a new experimental drug called phenylbutazone that was undergoing clinical trials but had not been approved by the Federal Drug Administration (FDA) or released to the public. It was a potent pain reliever and anti-inflammatory drug and was commonly used to treat racehorses.[5] The encouraging news was that Sandy Koufax, the all-star pitcher for the Los Angeles Dodgers, was quietly taking it with positive results.

I don't know how my doctor got a supply of "Bute," as it was known, and I chose not to ask.[6] When he handed me a month's supply, he warned that the drug was extremely risky. Potential side effects included both bone marrow and liver toxicity. Therefore, I needed to be tested each month to check my white blood cell count. In an "under-the-counter-like transaction," I walked away with renewed hope[7] and left for the Shenandoah Valley.

5. One year later, after winning the Kentucky Derby, Dancer's Image was disqualified when phenylbutazone was discovered in his bloodstream during the postrace urinalysis.

6. Later my doctor was arrested by federal authorities for defrauding Medicare out of three million dollars.

7. A few years after the trials, the FDA approved Bute, but later reversed the decision and outlawed it.

3

THE SUMMER OF '68

The summer of '68 was a time of social unrest. Peaceful civil rights protests gave way to violence in the streets. Much of it was precipitated by the April assassination of Martin Luther King Jr., the thirty-nine-year-old civil rights leader. Many inner-city residents, victims of high unemployment, slum housing, and prejudice, were now turning away from King's nonviolent philosophy and adopting more militant stances. "Black Power" became the new rallying cry. Stories and pictures of riots, looting, and violent confrontation with police filled the front pages of daily newspapers and weekly magazines.

The country was also in the throes of political chaos. The Vietnam War raged on, claiming the lives of thousands of American and Vietnamese soldiers. Walter Cronkite, anchor for CBS News, opened each broadcast by reporting the number of Americans killed in action that day. When President Lyndon Johnson unexpectedly announced he would not seek reelection, the Democratic nomination was up for grabs. Senator Robert Kennedy threw his hat in the ring and won both the South Dakota and California presidential primaries. After the Democrat standard-bearer delivered his victory speech in the Ambassador Hotel ballroom in Los Angeles on Wednesday, June 5, he exited through the hotel kitchen. Sirhan Sirhan, a hotel employee, stepped out of the crowd, aimed a pistol at the senator, and fired it, killing the popular candidate.

An FBI investigation later revealed that the assassin may have been in a self-induced trance at the time of the murder, since he claimed not to remember the incident. According to a *Time* magazine article, Sirhan spent hours in front of a mirror searching for his true identity and purpose in life.

> A mirror, two flickering candles, and Sirhan Sirhan. Alone in his cramped room, day after day, hour after silent hour, Sirhan studied Sirhan. Mail order courses in Rosicrucian mysticism had given him a new creed. They told [him] . . . that he could unlock from the mirror image . . . the inner knowledge, happiness and power he craved.
>
> Once instead of his own image in the mirror, Sirhan saw a vision of Robert Kennedy. . . .
>
> The candle swayed and changed color. . . . It was during one of these self-induced trances that Sirhan scribbled over and over again the words, "Kennedy must die! Kennedy must die!"[1]

For the first time, I realized that unstable souls might conjure up psychic forces. Whoa, that blew my mind!

THE SHENANDOAH VALLEY

On June 8, the day of Senator Kennedy's funeral, I departed for the Shenandoah Valley and three hours later pulled into the driveway of Claude Crawford, manager of the Craigsville Cardinals.[2] A former ma-

---

1. "Sirhan through the Looking Glass," *Time*, April 4, 1969, https://content.time.com/time/subscriber/article/0,33009,840003,00.html.
2. On the morning of my departure, I received an unexpected telegram from Paul Gravel, general manager of the Granby Baseball Club of the Canadian Provincial League, offering me four hundred dollars per month to play for his team. I still do not know how he got my name. I did not respond. I headed for the Valley League instead, hoping to work out my arm problems.

rine with a buzz cut and stern visage, he was an unhappy trooper when I knocked on his door at supper time. Managing the Cardinals was his summer job. The rest of the year he taught at a military academy in Staunton, Virginia, one of several such schools located throughout the Valley. He tossed me a team uniform and told me to follow him down the road to a log cabin where other rookies were staying. A few guys introduced themselves, but others just looked at me with suspicion, wondering if I were competing for their spot on the team.

As night fell, I had not yet eaten. One player directed me to a rickety one-room general store — the kind where old men sit around a coal stove and chew the fat. I walked down a narrow country road with no lights or sounds except those provided by the fireflies and crickets. I bought a Coke and a few candy bars. The next afternoon while taking infield practice, I was surprised I could throw the ball with only a twinge of pain in my shoulder. The Bute was working, but I knew things were not right.

Our game that evening against Harrisonburg was a disaster. The ballpark, the best facility in the league, was filled with boisterous fans who threw beer cans and hurled hostile epithets at our outfielders. The score was 12 to 1 in the seventh inning when the manager brought me off the bench to pinch-hit. I grounded out to shortstop. The fifty-mile bus ride back to Craigsville — along dark and winding roads — was miserable. We all sat in silence.

After a single game, I was ready to head home. I realized it was not worth the risk of getting bone marrow cancer or leukemia on the slim chance of being spotted by a scout. The next morning, I attached a note to my uniform and asked a player to return it to the manager. I headed home.

A Different Kind of Summer

I landed a summer job working as a playground director for the Baltimore County Bureau of Recreation and Parks. It was a refreshing change of pace. I worked with kids and taught them the importance of fair play and sportsmanship. Three nights a week, I played ball for the Spring Grove All Stars, whose roster included former minor leaguers and first-rate amateurs who for the love of the game continued to play into adulthood. For the first time in years, baseball was a pure joy. With no pressure to impress the scouts, I "tore the cover off the ball" and led the team in hitting. Frank Sansosti also arranged for me to catch batting practice for the Cleveland Indians whenever they came to play the Baltimore Orioles. It was fun suiting up, crouching behind home plate, and interacting with the players.

To relax I picked up a few more books on Olga's reading list. Two that stood out were written by Arthur Ford, the cofounder of the SFF. The first, *Nothing So Strange*, was an autobiography, telling of Ford's amazing spiritual journey, from his childhood in a fundamentalist home to becoming the world's best-known trance medium.[3] The second, *Unknown but Known*, updated his story and described Ford's meditative techniques for entering the trance state.[4] Both made for fascinating reading, and I soon discovered why many recognized Ford as the greatest trance medium of the twentieth century.

ARTHUR A. FORD

Arthur Augustus Ford was born 1897 in Titusville, Florida, the second of four children to a Southern Baptist mother and an Episcopal father. As a youngster — to his mother's delight — he was converted and baptized, but as a teenager he became intrigued with a Unitarian radio preacher who espoused anti-Trinitarianism and universal salvation for all. Leaders of the Baptist church called Ford on the carpet. When Ford refused to abandon the aberrant beliefs, the church board removed his name from the membership roll.

---

3. Arthur Ford with Margueritte Harmon Bro, *Nothing So Strange: The Autobiography of Arthur Ford* (New York: Harper & Sons, 1958).

4. Arthur Ford, *Unknown but Known: My Adventure into the Meditative Dimension* (New York: Harper & Row, 1968).

Despite the disciplinary action against him, Ford did not turn away from religion. He eventually joined the Disciples of Christ denomination and attended Transylvania College (Lexington, Kentucky), the denomination's school. In 1918, when World War I interrupted his education, Arthur enlisted in the army. While stationed at Camp Grant in Illinois, he began to have lucid dreams in which he heard voices whisper the names of soldiers killed in action. When the casualties were posted the next morning on the camp bulletin board, he read the names in his dreams. After the war, Arthur Ford returned to college and told a psychology professor about his experiences; the professor told Ford he had likely experienced psychic precognition. He encouraged his student to explore further this spiritual phenomenon.

As a pastoral studies major, Ford sought ordination in the Disciples of Christ and, upon graduation, accepted a call to pastor First Christian Church, Barbourville, Kentucky. While there, he met and married Sallie Stewart, a genuine "Kentucky belle." From 1921 to 1923 the church thrived under his leadership. Membership doubled, additional staff were hired, and a new educational wing was added.

Paul Pearson, the founder and president of the Swarthmore Chautauqua Association, was passing through Kentucky and happened to visit First Church. He was so impressed by Ford's sermon topic and ability to hold and move an audience that he invited the young man to join the Chautauqua circuit as a lecturer.[5]

In 1924, to the consternation of Sallie, Ford accepted the invitation and headed north. He never returned. His lecture "The Witching Hour" held audiences spellbound. He also developed a popular mind-reading act that he performed in New York, Massachusetts, and throughout New England.

Ford continued to explore psychic phenomena, especially spiritualism, a belief that it is possible for the living to contact the spirits of

5. Chautauqua was a movement and a cultural phenomenon that introduced popular musicians, speakers, preachers, entertainers, and adventurers to audiences living in the preindustrial centers of America in the late nineteenth and early twentieth centuries.

the dead through a human channel or medium. While in New York, he met Swami Paramhansa Yogananda, an Indian guru, who had migrated to the United States in order to introduce yogic meditation to Americans as a way of obtaining enlightenment. The swami taught Ford breathing techniques that allowed him to slip into a light trance.[6] In this heightened state of awareness, he claimed he was able to hear voices from the "other side" who informed him that they wished to contact their loved ones. Ford began holding public meetings in order to convey these messages. Hundreds gathered to receive a word from beyond the grave.

As Ford's fame grew in the mid-1920s, the First Spiritualist Church of New York invited him to preach regularly at its Sunday evening services in Carnegie Hall. Ford eventually assumed the role of pastor, which gave him a stable income and a sense of respectability. Under his leadership the congregation exploded in size. But his marriage to Sallie Stewart ended.

Employing new methods, Ford learned to enter deep trance that allowed departed spirits to enter his body and speak directly through his vocal cords. As his personality receded, theirs came forth. On one occasion a spirit identifying himself as Fletcher said he would serve as Ford's liaison to the spirit world from that day forward. As a result, Ford became the mouthpiece of Fletcher, who brought and interpreted messages to the living.

Three months after Harry Houdini's death on October 31, 1928, Ford announced that he had contacted the spirit of the world-famous magician. Prior to his passing, Houdini and his wife, Beatrice, had devised a secret code, known only to themselves. They agreed that upon the death of one spouse, the other would seek to make contact. To guard against fraud, the living spouse would ask the departed to repeat the code. Although many spiritualists said they communicated

6. Ford's claim notwithstanding, there is no extant evidence that he met or studied under the swami. In his book — Paramhansa Yogananda, *Autobiography of a Yogi* (New York: Philosophical Library, 1946) — Swami Yogananda does not mention Ford.

with Houdini, none was able to reveal the code. That is . . . until Arthur Ford knocked at Beatrice's door. The next day headlines across the country shouted, "Houdini Code Broken."

Ford found himself the focus of international attention. His fame grew exponentially. He traveled to England at the behest of Sir Arthur Conan Doyle, author of the Sherlock Holmes stories and an ardent spiritualist, who promoted Ford as the world's greatest trance medium. Over the years, Ford's clients included royalty from many countries, United States presidents, congressmen, and VIPs of all stripes, including author Fulton Oursler, humanitarian Sherwood Eddy, Pulitzer novelist Sinclair Lewis, and an array of the rich and famous.

In 1930, Ford was involved in a tragic automobile accident that killed his sister along with his best friend. An ambulance rushed Ford to the hospital, where he teetered between life and death. To relieve postoperative pain, his doctors prescribed morphine. By the time of his discharge, Ford was addicted. After a long struggle, Ford won his battle over drugs, but not over the persistent physical pain or the "survivor's guilt" that plagued him. He found solace in alcohol. With his health deteriorating, he sought help from Bill Wilson, the founder of Alcoholics Anonymous. They became lifelong friends.

The 1940s and '50s were transitional years for Arthur Ford. He continued to give trance readings but severed all relationships with spiritualist churches, whose reputation was sullied after several of their ministers were exposed as frauds and con artists. Reclaiming his Christian heritage, Ford limited his ministry to mainline churches. A man of simple tastes, Ford had little desire for material possessions and did not charge fees for his services. He lived alone in a Philadelphia apartment and traveled only to give lectures on the topic of life after death, pointing to Jesus's resurrection as proof of immortality. He drew large crowds, especially when he spoke at events sponsored by his beloved Spiritual Frontiers Fellowship.

In *Unknown but Known*, the sequel to *Nothing So Strange*, Ford tells how he again gained international notoriety in 1967 as the result of a séance he conducted for James Pike, the controversial Episcopal bishop.

A year earlier, Jim Jr., Pike's eldest son, took his own life. Suffering from extreme grief, depression, and guilt, Bishop Pike yearned to speak to his son just once more. Allen Spraggett, a Canadian writer and broadcaster, suggested Pike seek help from Arthur Ford. At a prearranged date and location, the two men met for the first time. After a few preliminary niceties and introductions, Ford moved to a recliner, placed a blindfold over his eyes, and started breathing deeply for several minutes before slipping into a trance. The bishop, sitting across from Ford, watched quietly and suspiciously. Suddenly Ford's lips began to quiver and made halting sounds as Fletcher took over and began to speak for Jim Jr. Bishop Pike asked several questions of his son, which Fletcher relayed to young Jim and then returned with answers. According to Pike, Fletcher conveyed personal information that only Pike and his son would have known. These private details convinced Bishop Pike that Ford had indeed contacted Jim.[7]

Spraggett videotaped the hour-long session and later aired it during prime time across Canada. Overnight, wire services picked up the story, and news of the séance spread around the world. Arthur Ford became a household name for the second time in his career. Thirty-eight years separated Ford's celebrated trance sessions for Houdini's widow and those for Bishop Pike.

When I began my journey in search of the supernatural, Arthur Ford was world famous. Some years later I would become friends with his most trusted protégé.

---

7. In his best-selling book *The Other Side*, Pike describes these events. James Pike with Diane Kennedy, *The Other Side: An Account of My Experiences with Psychic Phenomena* (Garden City, NY: Doubleday, 1968).

4

A FIFTH-YEAR SENIOR

The 1968–1969 school year was about to begin. I still needed twenty-one credits to complete my degree. As a fifth-year student, I was no longer eligible to play college baseball, but the athletic department offered to extend my scholarship if I was willing to serve as assistant coach of the Bees. I looked forward to this new role.

With a light academic schedule in the fall, I decided to audit a few evening courses at Baltimore School of the Bible to satisfy my newfound curiosity about Jesus. Dr. Funkhouser would have been proud. Located in a four-story townhouse in Bolton Hill (Baltimore's version of Georgetown in Washington, DC), the redbrick building housed four lecture halls, an auditorium, a library, offices, a book nook, and a break room. Founded in 1931 by several prominent ministers as a nondenominational school to teach people the basic tenets of the Christian faith, the school used local pastors and well-informed laypersons as professors. I signed up for three fifty-minute classes that met on Tuesday evenings. As a "sit-in," I was not required to take tests or write papers.

A twenty-minute chapel service was sandwiched between the first and second periods. About sixty to eighty students gathered to sing old hymns and listen to Jake Sheetz play upbeat gospel songs on his jazz saxophone. I would learn later that Jake was an icon in Baltimore religious circles. In the big band era, he was lead saxophonist in the popular Vincent Lopez orchestra.

In my short association with the Bible school, I came to appreciate these ordinary — mostly uneducated — people who unashamedly loved God and the Bible. Their simple faith was refreshing and contagious. I wanted what they had, but it somehow eluded me. The instructors encouraged us to "walk by faith" and "trust Jesus." When I asked them what they meant, they spoke in platitudes and were unable to offer clear-cut answers, which left me frustrated.

The whole time, I also continued my journey into parapsychology. I saw no contradiction between the two. I attended SFF meetings and read books on reincarnation, UFOs, mental telepathy, and the like.

A Visit to the Dean's Office

One afternoon I decided to drop by Dick Simms's office at the University of Baltimore. I wanted to tell him my story and seek advice. A former Methodist minister, Simms left the pastorate after a difficult divorce to become a professor of sociology and dean of students at the university. I took two of his classes and found him to be levelheaded and one of the most gracious persons I ever met.

The dean's office, enclosed by four panels of glass from floor to ceiling, faced the main student lounge, an enormous expanse with a checkered tile floor and gigantic white columns reaching the twenty-foot-high ceiling. Students filled the lounge daily to study, eat snacks, or shoot the breeze. Everyone could look directly into the dean's office. I was on full display!

After a few pleasantries, I poured my heart out to Dick Simms, not knowing how he might respond. *What will he think if I mention visiting a psychic healer, attending SFF meetings, auditing classes at the Bible school, or Dr. Funkhouser's call for his students' surrender to Christ?* To my relief, he didn't even blink an eye but listened with interest and empathy.

Simms encouraged me to continue my spiritual search. After a moment of reflection, he said, "Did you know that John Wesley, the founder of Methodism, took a path similar to yours? He had several paranormal experiences and prayed often without getting answers."

Then, almost as an afterthought he asked casually, "Have you ever considered going to seminary?"

I froze.

"Do you mean a place that trains ministers?"

"Yes, but seminary is also a good place to contemplate and find yourself."

Simms explained that he was a graduate of Wesley Theological Seminary (WTS) in Washington, DC, and said he was happy to make a few phone calls to see if they were still accepting applicants into their master of divinity program.

"I doubt they'll let me in," I said. "My grades aren't the best."

"Let me handle that problem," he replied.

I couldn't believe my ears. *Was seminary even an option?* As I walked out the door, Dick Simms asked me to drop by in a week or two. Maybe he'd have some news for me.

Before following up with him, I received a letter from the seminary registrar urging me to apply for admission.

I thought, "*This is insane!*" Nevertheless, in early November I filled out an application and mailed it back. To my utter surprise, I received a formal letter of acceptance on December 8, 1968, inviting me to become part of the incoming class the following fall. I was both excited and scared.

I was not prepared for what came next. Within a few weeks — out of the blue — I received a special delivery package postmarked Montreal, Quebec, Canada. Inside the large, padded envelope, I found a letter from Claude Bedard, general manager of the Quebec Indians Baseball Club, inviting me to play for his team in the Canadian Provincial League. A contract for five hundred dollars per month was attached. My heart skipped a beat. I couldn't believe what was happening! Without hesitation or forethought, I signed and returned the contract to Mr. Bedard. Were my lifelong hopes becoming a reality?

Almost immediately, I knew I had made a mistake. I would now have to start back on a regimen of phenylbutazone. Yikes! Although it might take away my pain, I realized it could not heal my arm. And what about attending seminary? The baseball season and the seminary semester overlapped; I couldn't do both.

I decided to kick the can down the road and deal with the situation later. In the meantime, I needed to pass my courses and fulfill my scholarship obligation as the Bees assistant coach.

I spent every afternoon in the spring of 1969 hitting infield practice; during games I coached first base. The Bees were thin on talent and finished a disappointing second in the league.

Finally, the day arrived that I dreaded most. I received another special delivery package that included immigration papers, a plane reservation to Montreal, and instructions to report to the Quebec Indians in two weeks' time. With great trepidation, I lifted the phone and called Claude Bedard. With regrets I told him I would not be coming but had decided instead to attend seminary. At first, he attempted to change my mind. When that tactic failed, he became livid and reminded me in no uncertain terms that I was in breach of my contract. After an exchange of sharp words, the call ended abruptly.[1] We never talked again.[2]

✦

To earn money that summer for seminary, I sold trophies to sports teams to cover my upcoming expenses. I also made a short pilgrimage to Virginia Beach, the popular ocean resort and home of the ARE, Edgar Cayce's organization. Located on Atlantic Avenue, a few miles north of the tourist attractions, hotels, eateries, arcades, and gifts shops, the ARE sits high atop a sand dune, only a few hundred feet

1. The reason Bedard was so angry when I refused to play for his club was because he had traded a player to obtain my contract from the Granby Cardinals. Unbeknownst to me, the year before, on the recommendation of scout Frank Sansosti, the Cardinals had placed me on their roster.

2. Over the next few years, I continued to play summer ball for sport and occasionally caught batting practice for the Cleveland Indians and the Detroit Tigers when they were in town to play the Baltimore Orioles. It was fun, but baseball had lost its luster.

from the shoreline. I toured the immaculate grounds; attended lectures on reincarnation, prophecy, and dreams; and had interesting conversations with staff and visitors.

As the summer ended, I faced an unknown future as a seminary student. I had never stepped foot on a seminary campus and had no idea what to expect. My imagination ran wild.

Will everyone be walking around like monks in flowing robes with heads bowed and hands folded in prayer?

The thought was frightening and unsettling.

What have I gotten myself into?

I will never fit in.

I wanted to run away. But where would I go? The Vietnam War was getting hotter by the day. And although no Major League team had drafted me, I knew Uncle Sam would not miss the chance! At least as a seminary student I was beyond the reach of the Selective Service Board.

So, I reluctantly packed my bags, said my good-byes, left my old life behind, and headed to Washington, DC.

5

WASHINGTON, DC

Our nation's capital is unlike any other city in America. One never tires of spotting a presidential motorcade or looking upon the majestic white marble edifices dedicated to Washington, Jefferson, Lincoln, and other stalwarts who formed our country into a bastion of Western civilization.

Wesley Theological Seminary is located on Massachusetts Avenue in an upscale neighborhood in northwest Washington and sits atop ten manicured acres next to the American University, a sister institution. Embassy Row, the National Cathedral, and the Naval Observatory (home to the vice president) are all within walking distance.

The seminary was not like I had imagined. The beautiful campus of redbrick buildings housed classrooms, offices, dorms, married-student apartments, a lovely chapel, and a refectory with wall-to-wall windows that looked out on a lush green pastoral landscape with tall pines and an impressive statue of John Wesley, the father of Methodism, astride his faithful steed.

After checking in with the registrar and receiving my room assignment, I attended an orientation meeting led by L. Harold DeWolf, the new dean of faculty. A well-known theologian and author, De-Wolf came to Wesley after a long career at Boston University, where he served as Martin Luther King Jr.'s PhD dissertation supervisor and later became his confidant.[1] After greeting the incoming class, DeWolf introduced the Wesley faculty, several of whom were scholars of note with degrees from Harvard, Yale, Boston, Duke, Chicago, and Basel. Turning his attention back to us, DeWolf declared, "Wesley is not a *Bible school* that seeks to indoctrinate students but a place of deep theological reflection and open debate."

At a student reception, I learned that most of the entering classmates came from Methodist backgrounds and were preparing for pulpit ministry. Very few, however, had even a cursory knowledge of the Scriptures but leaned more toward liberalism in both theology and politics. The campus was a continuous hubbub of activity. It was not uncommon for students to join antiwar protests or throw their support behind a liberal candidate for local and national office.

During my first semester, I signed up for a few traditional courses in theology and church history, but I spent most of my time making friends with those who would rather hang out at a local barroom than the campus library.

Wesley, on the progressive end of theological education, did not require one to take a core set of courses to graduate but allowed each student to design his or her own curriculum. This suited me just fine. When the second semester (spring 1970) rolled around, I signed up for "Mysticism, East and West," one among many courses offered that focused on world religions, cults, and religious sects. The professor, J. H. Pyke (no relation to Bishop Pike), a former foreign missionary to China, had established friendly relationships with Hindu, Buddhist, Sufi, Baha'i, and Shinto leaders, as well as many psychic practitioners.

In the late 1960s and 1970s, the District of Columbia was a hotbed of occult and paranormal activities. Many psychic and cult leaders gravitated to the city to gain access to the powerful and mighty.

---

1. DeWolf was the only white man invited to speak at Martin Luther King Jr.'s funeral service.

Among the more famous was Jeane Dixon, the "Washington Seeress" who served as a psychic advisor to every president from Franklin Roosevelt to Richard Nixon.

Each week Dr. Pyke took our class on a field trip to visit a religious group or had a representative of a religious group come to campus to lecture us.

On one occasion we crossed the District line into Bethesda, Maryland, to tour the Self-Revelation Church of Absolute Monism. Better known as the Golden Lotus Temple, the "church" was founded in 1928 by Swami Prenananda, a disciple of the famed Swami Yogananda, the man who first introduced yoga to America and, according to Arthur Ford, taught him how to enter a trance. A staff member wearing an immaculate white robe and a Nehru collar greeted us. Achariya Peter was thirty-something with coifed jet-black hair, a bright smile, pleasant demeanor, and brilliant mind.

ACHARIYA PETER

Peter shared his story of how he became a Hindu priest. He was born Peter Donner in 1935 in Berlin, Germany, during Adolf Hitler's ascent to power. His affluent Lutheran family refused to support the deranged führer or his Nazi Party. When Hitler's Storm Troopers launched their vicious attack on the Jewish population in November 1938, over 7,500 Jewish businesses were destroyed, 25,000 people arrested, and 267 synagogues burned to the ground.[2] Things worsened when Hitler invaded Poland and eventually carted off countless numbers of Jews to concentration camps and gas chambers.

In desperation, Peter's family took decisive action. They sent their five-year-old son to boarding school in southern Germany. He never saw his parents again!

When Peter turned eleven, the International Red Cross arranged for a German-speaking Lutheran family from South Carolina to adopt

---

2. This horrific event was known as *Kristallnacht*, "night of broken glass."

the orphaned boy and bring him to America where he could find some semblance of stability. After high school he matriculated to Middlebury University (Vermont) and earned his BA degree. While on campus, he sought answers to life's most difficult questions, including the source of evil, the reason for the Holocaust, and the nature of man, as well as personal issues such as the death of his parents and his own dissatisfaction in life. In the end, he believed that Brahmanism, an advanced form of Hinduism, offered the best answers.

Peter decided to move to his home country and attend the University of Mainz, where he earned his MA degree. Upon returning to America, he settled in Washington, DC, got a job, married, began a family, officially abandoned his Lutheran faith, and joined the Golden Lotus Temple. In 1968, Peter renounced married life and embraced celibacy. He dropped his given name, took the moniker Achariya Peter, and accepted ordination as a Brahman priest in the Golden Lotus Temple.

During our visit to the temple, Peter not only shared his remarkable story but gave us a tour of the temple grounds, with their beautiful gardens and a reflecting pool. His extraordinary hospitality put us all at ease. As we relaxed and enjoyed pastries and refreshments, Peter casually explained that absolute monism acknowledges the oneness of God, which he noted was the foundation of all advanced religions. He also emphasized the oneness of all things (pantheism) but said most people fail to recognize this profound truth because our senses are limited and distort reality.

According to Peter, *yoga* (a Sanskrit word meaning union) is the means of transcending our senses and reaching the state of self-realization or oneness with creation. He emphasized that this does not happen overnight. Only as we remain on this yogic path do we eventually become aware that our soul (Atman) and God (Brahman) are not separate entities but of one essence. Peter used the Christian term "at-one-ment" to describe this reality and quoted Jesus's own words, "I and my Father are one."

On our ride back to campus, my classmates engaged in a lively conversation, and we all agreed Achariya Peter was very winsome and persuasive. A few students steeped in church history and theology, however, were critical of Peter's pantheistic beliefs and wondered how he could discard Lutheranism for Eastern mysticism. After all, Peter's native land was the birthplace of Luther and the Protestant Reformation. Lutheran pastors and scholars like Dietrich Bonhoeffer and Martin Niemöller of the Confessing Church spoke out against Hitler, the very man responsible for the death of Peter's parents. Why would Peter abandon the very church that fought against the evils of the Holocaust? We asked Dr. Pyke his opinion, but he just smiled and kept driving.

Pyke wanted to expose us to the different forms of religious faith and let us make up our own minds what to believe. That was fine with me.

WTS uniquely provided me with many opportunities to meet and interact with mainstream and fringe religious leaders, including those associated with the Unification Church (the Moonies), ISCKON (Hare Krishnas), International Meditation Society for the Science of Creative Intelligence (Transcendental Meditation), Sufism (mystical form of Islam), Scientology, and others.

For me the highlight of the semester was a visit from William Theodore (Ted) Swager, an ordained Methodist minister and trance medium. After being introduced, the thirty-eight-year-old Swager stepped behind the lectern, smiled broadly, and said he wanted to tell some ghost stories. We all laughed. Swager felt right at home in the classroom, and no wonder. Only ten years before he had sat in these same chairs as an MDiv student.

TED SWAGER

Ted had taught high school and coached varsity football in Pennsylvania for several years. After much counsel, he resigned and entered WTS as a twenty-eight-year-old married student. Ed Bauman, professor of pastoral theology and senior pastor of Foundry United Methodist Church, introduced Ted to the occult. Bauman announced he was hosting an evening meeting at his home with Irene Hughes of Chicago, one of America's leading psychics. Students could earn extra credit if they attended. Swager was one of a few students to show up.

After preliminary introductions and some small talk, the group was asked to sit in a circle of chairs surrounding Ms. Hughes. She spoke for a few minutes and then slipped into a semitrance. In this altered state she addressed each person. When she got to Swager, she took his hand and spoke of his childhood, describing his house, friends, and areas of interest. She then gave him a message from his departed father. After pausing, she said, "Ted, you have psychic ability. Develop it."

Ted didn't know what to think. The whole evening seemed unreal. He was both confused and excited. Professor Bauman suggested that Ted join the Washington chapter of the SFF, which he did. Arthur Ford, one of its founders, came through town to speak. His topic was immortality of the soul and the ability to speak with the dead, which he equated with the "communion of saints," a cherished Christian belief and an essential part of the Apostles' Creed.

After his lecture, Ford conducted a private sitting for a small group of people who stayed behind. Ted was one of them. The spirit of Fletcher, speaking through Ford's vocal cords, confirmed that Ted possessed psychic ability. As a result, Ted and Ford kept in touch and eventually became good friends.

After graduation from seminary, Ted was ordained as an elder and became pastor of Calvary United Methodist Church in Waldorf, Maryland. On several occasions Ford visited Ted's church and witnessed healings as Swager laid hands on the sick.

Recognizing Ted's psychic potential, Ford invited Ted to meet with him each week at his Philadelphia apartment in the Westbury Hotel. For two years, Ted traveled to Philadelphia and spent Friday and part of Saturday with Ford, who taught him how to enter a trance and speak to the dead.

In *Unknown but Known*, Ford extolled Swager's abilities as a medium. As a result, people from all over the nation flocked to Waldorf to have sittings with Ted. In March 1968, Ted Swager was named chairman of the Washington, DC, chapter of the SFF. Under his leadership, membership exploded. Ted spoke regularly at SFF meetings and in churches up and down the East Coast and throughout Middle America. He conducted trance sittings for ordinary people as well as for governors, congresspeople, and presidential hopefuls.[3]

In the summer of 1968, Ben Bradlee, editor of the *Washington Post*, his wife Toni, and her brother-in-law, *Newsweek* reporter Jim Truitt, contacted Ted for a reading. They were seeking information on the unsolved murder of Toni's sister Mary Pinchot Meyer, who was shot to death in Rock Creek Park four years earlier. The trio hoped to contact Mary's spirit. When the *New York Times* got wind of the story and identified Ted Swager as the medium, Ben Bradlee was livid.

Mary Pinchot Meyer, a well-known artist and Georgetown socialite, was the former wife of Cord Meyer, a highly ranked CIA officer. Her two-year love affair with President John F. Kennedy was an open secret in elite circles. Unlike JFK's other lovers, Meyer was his intellectual equal, and the two spent many long nights discussing politics, experimenting with drugs, and frolicking in the bedroom. JFK's untimely death ended the tryst. On the morning of October 12, 1964, less than a year after the president's assassination, Mary was shot and killed as she jogged along a wooded towpath. The police quickly arrested a derelict and charged him with the crime, but he was later acquitted. The case remained unsolved.

Circumstances surrounding Mary's mysterious death didn't add up. Police did not find a weapon and ruled out robbery as a motive. Even more disconcerting was the location of two clean bullet wounds — one in the temple and the other in the back. The coroner suggested the killer was likely well trained in the use of firearms. Some believed she was the victim of a CIA hit.[4]

---

3. Among the more noted visitors were Iowa senator Harold Hughes, Michigan congressman Gerald Ford, and Washington prophetess Jeane Dixon.

4. Peter Janney, *Mary's Mosaic: The CIA Conspiracy to Murder John F. Kennedy, Mary Pinchot Meyer, and Their Vision for World Peace*, 3rd ed. (New York: Skyhorse Publishing, 2013), 55.

Within hours of her death, Ben and Toni Bradlee stopped by Mary's townhouse and discovered James Jesus Angleton, director of counterintelligence for the CIA, rooting through her personal effects and grasping her private diary, where she possibly kept notes of her affair. Startled and agitated by the unexpected interruption, Angleton left the scene. Mary's diary was never seen again.

Seeking more information on the murder, the Bradlees and Truitt turned to Swager for answers. Unfortunately, no recording exists of the session, and we may never know what Swager revealed.[5] But according to Truitt, Swager slipped into a trance and contacted Mary. Truitt wrote that the information received was helpful and "remarkable."[6]

As Swager's reputation grew, people from across the country began to call and request appointments for sittings.[7]

In his lecture to our class, Ted Swager did not mention the Mary Meyer affair. He mainly spoke of his own spiritual journey from seminary student to trance medium and how Arthur Ford befriended and mentored him. He also announced that he had recently left the pastorate, formed a nonprofit organization (the Spiritual Center for Healing, Counseling, and Parapsychology), and purchased a beautiful property in Fairhaven, Maryland, along the shoreline of the Chesapeake Bay, to serve as his headquarters.[8]

I sat spellbound as Swager told his story. He characterized his work as a *Christian* ministry and peppered his talk with quotes from the

5. Swager confirmed that he conducted a séance for the Bradlees and Truitt at his church in Waldorf, but refused to reveal any details. See David Cowan, "Former Minister Finds New Faith," *Carroll County (Westminster, MD) Times*, March 15, 1976.

6. See Nina Burleigh, *A Very Private Woman: The Life and Unsolved Murder of Presidential Mistress Mary Meyer* (New York: Bantam Books, 1998), 303–4. Also see "People," *Time*, March 8, 1976, 42, for Truitt's recollection of the séance.

7. SFF Newsletter 5, no. 10 (May 1969).

8. SFF Newsletter 3, no. 10 (October 1, 1969). Ted moved to Fairhaven, which was located about thirty-five miles east of Washington, DC, and offered easy access for the many politicians and other important movers and shakers who sought Ted's otherworldly guidance.

Scriptures. From his point of view, he was continuing in the tradition of Jesus and the apostles.

The class ended at 11:30 a.m., and most of my classmates made a beeline for the door. I hung back, introduced myself, and asked Swager if he had time for lunch. Ted was surprised by my knowledge of psychic phenomena. I told him about my arm injury, meeting with Olga, the reading list, and my pilgrimage to the ARE. We quickly discovered we were kindred spirits. We sat in the seminary refectory and talked for three hours before Ted had to leave to beat the afternoon traffic out of Washington. As we said our good-byes, Ted invited me to visit the Spiritual Center.

As soon as I got back to my dorm room, I found a copy of Ford's *Unknown but Known* on my bookshelf, turned to the index, and found Ted's name listed several times on pages 149–51. Here Ford writes of Swager's initial interest in spiritualism, his weekly trips to Philly, and Ford's visits to Ted's church. Ford concludes his section on Ted with a strong endorsement, stating that Ted's "natural gifts are great" and that he "will be heard from."

I couldn't believe I was now friends with Ted Swager, protégé of the world's most respected trance medium. I planned to hitch my wagon to Swager's rising star.

6

MY FIRST SÉANCE

I considered my first year of seminary a success. With the summer of '70 at hand, I wanted to take up Ted Swager's invitation to visit the Spiritual Center. We set a date.

As I drove from my home in Baltimore to Fairhaven, I could only imagine what the meeting held in store. I exited the main highway and followed the map's directions to a county road that continued for several miles to a dead end. I turned left, drove a few hundred yards, and spotted the entrance.

A long gravel driveway led up to a three-story redbrick colonial mansion situated on a pristine estate overlooking the Chesapeake Bay. Because of its strategic location, it was convenient for clients living in Washington, only a thirty-five-minute drive to the east. Ted spotted my red Chevy II and came out to greet me. It was like a reunion of sorts. The smell of the bay filled the air. After he gave me a quick tour of the center, we spent our time together on the large screened-in porch at the back of the house, drank iced tea, and caught up since our last meeting. Ted wanted to know about my studies and nostalgically asked about the Wesley faculty. I had dozens of questions about the nature of psychic gifts (he thought they were from God), reincarnation (he didn't believe in it), world religions (he said he was a Christian and served Jesus, but all religions possessed some truth), and other deep and sundry topics. The visit lasted about two hours.

As I got up to leave, I suggested halfheartedly that maybe one day I could study under Ted as he had with Arthur Ford. He only smiled and said, "Let's take a stroll."

We walked the length of the property with its tall shade trees and plenty of open spaces. Ted pulled his pipe from his shirt pocket, lit it, and proceeded to tell me the amazing story of how he came to purchase the estate.

The realtor who showed him the property said it once belonged to the Russian embassy. Diplomats and other high-ranking officials working in Washington used it as a weekend retreat from the hustle and bustle of the city. *If only the walls could speak!*

The asking price was far beyond Ted's means. He asked the realtor for a few minutes to be alone. As he walked toward the outer perimeter of the property, he heard a voice coming from behind: *Buy it.* He turned but saw no one. He took a few more steps and again heard the words, *Buy it.* Believing this to be divine guidance, he returned and made an offer substantially less than the asking price. The realtor said the owner would not entertain such a "lowball" figure. Believing God wanted him to set up his ministry at Fairhaven, Ted convinced the realtor, despite her misgivings, to submit it.

"Al, God works in *mysterious ways*," he chuckled. "Who knows, maybe he does have a place for you at the Spiritual Center."

When I got in my car to leave, my head was spinning.

I returned to the Spiritual Center two more times that summer, the first to attend a Sunday afternoon worship service. Ted kept his ordination credentials and considered himself a Methodist minister. Every week a group of thirty to forty people gathered in the club basement of the center for worship. The service was simple and not out of the ordinary: Scripture reading, a few hymns, a sermon, and prayers for the sick. According to my notes, Ted preached on Hebrews 12:1–2.

I was surprised, however, that Ted did not mention a word about psychic gifts or mediumship during the service, and I asked him about it later.

"Al," he explained, "a lot of people are curiosity seekers. Jesus spoke about those who search for miracles but have no interest in seeking God."

Before heading back to Baltimore, I joined the others for lunch and good conversation. Ted played his guitar and we sang a few choruses. He seemed happy in his pastoral role.

To be quite frank, I was more like the people Jesus condemned. I was interested in Ted's psychic powers and, as a result, drove away from Fairhaven somewhat disappointed.

I spent most of my summer relaxing, reading, going to SFF meetings, and catching batting practice for the Cleveland Indians and the Detroit Tigers whenever they were in town. Occasionally, my mother and I would make a trek downtown for lunch at the Palmer House, a Baltimore institution where the price of lunch included a card reading by Alma, a well-known psychic.

Speaking to the Dead

Before returning to seminary for the new fall semester, I arranged a trance reading with Ted. He crowded me into a busy schedule and suggested I bring along a few friends. Five of us headed for Fairhaven — Charles, a fellow seminarian; my mother, Jean Streett; her best friend, Mrs. Garner; her friend's mother, Mrs. Spinks; and I. We talked and laughed the whole way there.

Ted, dressed in a casual shirt and slacks, greeted us at the front door, invited us inside, and introduced his wife, Lois. My companions and I had no idea what to expect. This was the first séance any of us had attended. We assembled in a great room with bookcases lining two walls, from floor to ceiling. Along the back wall were several large windows that looked out onto Chesapeake Bay. Swager's sons were playing in the backyard, and I heard their dog barking as it chased them. Five folding chairs were arranged in a semicircle, and Lois asked us to take a seat. An empty recliner sat in front of us. A small wooden table with a Wollensak reel-to-reel tape recorder was on our left, and Lois next to it. After a few pleasantries Ted excused himself and Lois explained what to expect. She said, "In a moment Ted will return, take a seat in the recliner, and start to meditate until he slips into trance. At some point, his spirit guides will begin to speak."

Ted returned shortly and did exactly as Lois had described. He sat down, smiled at us, and then placed a folded silk handkerchief over his eyes and tied it in the back. After adjusting his body comfortably in the chair, he began to take deep, long breaths — in and out, in and out. The breathing slowed with each inhale and exhale and became less audible. This continued for ten or fifteen minutes, but it seemed to be much longer. As I sat quietly and nervously, my imagination ran wild, anticipating what would happen next. Then, suddenly and without warning, Ted slumped over in the recliner and didn't move. It looked like he was about to fall onto the floor, and I reached out to grab him, but Lois raised her hand and stopped me.

"Al, don't touch him. Right now, Ted is very vulnerable. He has departed his body."

I looked around and everyone was on pins and needles. Then just as suddenly as before, Ted took one long breath and sat up. His face seemed a little distorted, and his lips quivered as words formed in his mouth. At first, he spoke slowly and haltingly.

"Hello . . . Hello . . ."

My guests and I sat frozen in our seats. We didn't know how to react.

Lois encouraged us: "The spirits are greeting you. Welcome them into your midst."

We hesitantly and awkwardly replied, "Hello," but our words were nearly inaudible as they stuck in our throats.

Despite being self-conscious, we eventually loosened up and peppered Swager with questions about personal decisions, world affairs, the Vietnam War, and a host of theological issues.

Two spirits used Ted's voice to communicate. One, identified as BS, answered questions related to theology and religious matters. The other, known as BA, addressed inquiries about personal and mundane matters. Throughout the trance, Ted's voice never changed, and it was not possible to tell which spirit spoke, except by the subject matter at hand.

I later learned in private conversations with Ted that BA was a male relative who influenced him in his youth. The other, BS, was Alexander Preston Shaw, the first African American minister appointed bishop in the Methodist church at the age of seventy-one. Ted trusted both to speak through him.

The ninety-minute sitting was recorded (I now wish I had a copy). A few exchanges between BS and me still stand out. I offer them as best I can remember.

BS: You have lived before as a New England pastor.

Me: *Do you mean I have been reincarnated?*

BS: Yes, you were a dry preacher and bored your congregation to death (he followed this comment with a slight laugh). You have now returned to preach a message that will bring life to all who hear it.

Me: *Do you mean I will pastor a local church?*

BS: No, you will be a well-known evangelist and speak to thousands.

Me: *What else do you wish to say about my future?*

BS: What John Wesley learned; you will come to learn also.[1]

Me: *Is Jesus the only way to salvation?*

BS: Christ is the perfect master who leads us to God.

---

1. Upon reflection, I remembered the story of John Wesley's return by ship to England after his failed missionary efforts in America. He said, "I came to save the Indians, but who will save me?" Onboard he met Peter Bohler, a Moravian minister, who advised Wesley "to preach faith until you have faith." Like Wesley, I prayed daily and asked Christ into my heart, but nothing seemed to change. Maybe this was the lesson I needed to learn.

Me: *What about other religions?*

BS: They too lead to God. But Jesus, known as the Christ,
is the more perfect way. He showed mortals how to live
according to love. The degree we walk in this light will
determine our position in the next life.

Me: *Which life do you mean — in heaven or on the earth?*

BS: We must first work off our karma until we master the
way of Christ. This can take many earthly incarnations.
Then we move through heavenly realms until we attain
God consciousness.

Me: *Will Jesus Christ return to earth a second time?*

BS: His spirit is already in the world, but the world does not
recognize him.

Me: *But will Christ personally return again?*[2]

BS: The second coming as you call it will occur, but not as you
understand it. The full arrival of the Christ shall fill the
earth and the new age will begin.

        *Before I could ask another question, BA interrupted and ad-
dressed Mrs. Garner.*

BA: Young lady, when your husband was twelve years old, he
became very ill. Everyone thought it was appendicitis. Is
that correct?

Mrs. G: I didn't know my husband at that time, and he never mentioned it to me.

BA: He was rushed to the hospital, and they discovered an
infection of some kind. Is that correct?

Mrs. G: I've not heard that story before.

BA: Well, it is correct. Check it out. [The spirit became somewhat agitated at Mrs. Garner and spoke in an authoritative tone.]

---

2. I asked this question based on what I learned at the Baltimore School of
the Bible.

> *Then BA brought a personal message that struck an emotional nerve but never identified the intended recipient.*

BA: Yes, I have an older soul here. [The spirit did not provide a name.]

BA: He says, "It's okay." He knows you had to do it. He says, "I love you and forgive you."

The words caused Mrs. Spinks to let out an audible gasp. We all looked at her. She was white as a ghost.

The sitting continued, and we asked many more questions covering philosophy, world affairs, and health. A few attempts were made to contact a deceased brother-in-law who died of lung cancer while in the prime of life and a father who passed away when the sitter was a small child, but no connection was made. The whole while, Mrs. Spinks remained silent and wiped away an occasional tear.

As Ted's energy seemed to wane, his cadence slowed and he simply bowed his head in silence. After a few minutes, Ted took a long, cleansing breath and was back among us. He gradually removed his blindfold and sat quietly like a person who had just woken from sleep. Then he smiled and said he hoped everything went well. We nodded.

Just as unceremoniously as we had been ushered inside, Ted thanked us for coming, we said our good-byes, and departed. As soon as we got into the car, we all burst into laughter. My friend Charles and my mother were the first to speak. Both were skeptical and postulated that Ted was awake the whole time.

My blood boiled at their disbelief: "Why would Ted put on an act for ninety minutes?" It didn't make sense to me.

I turned to Mrs. Spinks, who sat pensive in the back, and asked, "What about you? What do you think?"

Her eyes glistened as tears formed and then ran down her cheeks. "I know it is real. Mr. Swager brought me a message from Henry."

"Who is Henry?" I inquired.

"Henry is my late husband."

Her answer caught me off guard.

"As we grew old together," she said, "we agreed that if either ever became gravely ill or incapacitated, the other would care for them at home. But I broke my promise and placed Henry in a facility."

By this time, she was sobbing into her handkerchief.

Gaining her composure, this gentle older lady let out a sigh. "Oh, don't mind me. I'm a mess. But I actually feel relieved."

For Mrs. Spinks, the session melted away years of guilt.

A strange and awkward silence filled the car. Charles stared out the passenger window. My mother fiddled nervously with her purse. Mrs. Garner, sitting next to her mom, cried and hugged her. And I tried to drive, but the lines on the road suddenly seemed blurry.

PART 2

7

THE GREAT REVERSAL

My second year at Wesley brought immediate changes. I was offered a part-time pastor's position at Curtis Bay United Methodist Church in South Baltimore. Although I feared public speaking
and had never written or delivered a sermon, I accepted the offer,
knowing this would fulfill a graduation requirement.[1]

The church building, with its four white columns, sat on a hill at
a main crossroads and towered over the quaint houses, barrooms, and
ethnic clubs that dotted the streets of this blue-collar neighborhood.
Curtis Bay is located on an inlet of the Patapsco River and is the home
of the United States Coast Guard shipyard.

To look presentable on my first Sunday, I bought a three-piece
black suit at an upscale secondhand shop. On September 10, 1970,
I walked into the pulpit and faced the sixty or so parishioners who
came to meet and greet their new minister.

---

1. WTS required all divinity students to serve in a church for a least one
year before graduation.

THE MAKING OF AN EVANGELIST

With no previous preaching experience, I decided to use Billy Graham as my role model, emulating his delivery and mannerisms, even punching the air with my forefinger for emphasis. For sermon material, I copied pages out of two of his books, *Peace with God* and *World Aflame*, changing only a few words here and there to reflect my limited vocabulary.[2] I preached one chapter a week. On Saturday evenings, I practiced reading my manuscript aloud in front of a mirror, and on Sunday mornings I arrived early and practice-preached to an empty sanctuary. When the service began, I was ready.

At the close of each sermon, like Graham, I called for parishioners to step forward and give themselves to Christ. To my surprise, they responded! Kneeling at the altar, they prayed and cried out for forgiveness as the weight of their sins lifted. Many lives were changed: alcoholics gave up the bottle, marriages were restored, and students stopped cheating.

Although I rejoiced with these converts, I was jealous and wanted what they had. For two years I had prayed nightly for Christ to come into my life as Dr. Funkhouser had urged, but peace eluded me.

After exhausting Billy Graham's books for sermon content, I freaked out. *Where will I find more material for next week's sermon?* In desperation, I turned to my old notes from the Baltimore School of the Bible and somehow cobbled together a pitiful message.

As I stepped into the pulpit, my heart raced and my knees nearly buckled, but when I opened my mouth, I suddenly felt weightless, like I was floating a foot off the ground. Time stood still. Since no one said they saw me hover, I assume nothing seemed out of the ordinary — at least, to them! For the next several weeks the same thing happened. Then one Sunday everything returned to normal, and from that day forward I no longer feared speaking in public.

---

2. Billy Graham, *Peace with God* (New York: Doubleday, 1953), and *World Aflame* (New York: Doubleday, 1963).

Despite my new confidence in the pulpit, my life was in shambles. Since my days of playing college baseball, I had been a heavy drinker. Road trips and long hours on the team bus provided opportunities to indulge. Players usually stocked up on liquor before heading off to "away games." By the time we arrived, it was a wonder we could take the field, much less win a game. But we did! I continued to drink heavily during seminary and found like-minded classmates who enjoyed imbibing as well. On many nights, we closed down the barroom before heading back to campus.

The school year flew by at breakneck speed. Between my responsibilities as a student and pastor, and hanging out with my drinking buddies, I had little time for much else.

I stayed in touch with my friend Ted Swager, but only by phone calls and short notes. As his fame spread, requests for trance readings increased. He now had weekly sittings scheduled for two years out.

CONVERSION

In the fall semester of 1971, I took "Contemporary Theology" under Dr. Ed Bauman, the same professor who years earlier introduced Ted Swager to spiritualism. Besides serving a large church, Bauman hosted the Emmy award–winning *Bauman Bible Telecast*. A tall man with deep, dark eyes, a wiry frame, and magnetic personality, Bauman was a dynamo in the classroom and a favorite among students. I could never have anticipated his impact on my life.

Bauman was a disciple of Paul Tillich, the well-respected but controversial German theologian. To illustrate Tillich's unique view of salvation, Bauman used the marker board. At the top he wrote the word "God," and at the bottom, the word "man," leaving a large gap between the two words. Pointing to the empty space, he said, "We all feel alienated or separated from God."

I can still see the board in my mind's eye. Dr. Bauman next drew a large cross in the space connecting the words "God" and "man" and said, "Christ has closed the gap, and as a result, each of us is *now* reconciled to God."

Excitedly he proclaimed, "This is good news!"

If that's the case, I thought, *why do I still feel separated from God?*

As if anticipating my question, Bauman explained, "Even though we are reconciled already, many of us don't realize it; so, we continue striving for God, who already accepts us." Then he paraphrased Tillich: "We must simply accept the fact that we are accepted."

That was my problem. I could not believe God accepted me. I was a borderline drunk, a hypocrite, and a faker. Surely, I had to change *before* he accepted me.

Had my parishioners known the *real* Alan Streett, they would have likely tossed me out on my ear. Or if Dr. Pyke, my favorite professor, knew what I was really like, he would have been disappointed.

I lived in constant fear of being exposed!

My parents, who knew me best, wondered why I attended seminary in the first place and how I had the audacity to preach.

Worse yet, each morning when I looked in the mirror, I didn't like what I saw. I wanted to change but didn't have the power to make it happen.

Bauman's assertion that God knew me — flaws and all — and yet unconditionally accepted me was overwhelming. I left the classroom in a daze, walked back to my dorm room, and fell into my overstuffed chair. I can't explain rationally what happened next, but reaching the end of my rope, I cried out, "Oh God, help me!"

Suddenly the floodgates of heaven opened, and God's love poured into the room and enveloped me. Unable to move, I sat paralyzed for nearly two hours and wept openly. Immersed in God's presence, I knew everything was going to be all right. When God's Spirit lifted, the alienation was gone. Transformed and filled with joy, I was beaming from ear to ear.[3] Fellow students noticed a marked difference in my countenance and asked, "What happened to you?" I told them.

As word spread across campus, a few classmates whom I hardly knew stopped by my dorm room to say how excited they were for

3. I discovered that the key to having a relationship with God did not come by repeating a formulaic prayer but by surrendering one's will to God.

me. They called themselves "evangelicals." Tom Short, John Secret, Harley Krause, and I started hanging out and eventually became good friends. They invited me to attend the Tuesday night worship service at a church just a few blocks from the campus.

"I never heard of a church that meets on Tuesday," I said.

"This is a different kind of church. It's a charismatic church."

I was aware of the Jesus movement sweeping the land, composed mainly of former hippies and college dropouts who now followed Jesus, but I was not familiar with the charismatic movement.

Christ Church met not only on Tuesdays but on several nights a week! Speakers from around the world would visit to preach, teach, and tell of their own supernatural encounters with the Holy Spirit.[4]

I did not know what to expect. Boy, was I ever in for a surprise!

---

4. Derek Prince, a Bible teacher from Great Britain with an Eton pedigree, spoke often. David du Plessis, a South African known as "Mr. Pentecost," was a regular. He told of how God opened doors for him to share the message of Pentecost with the leaders of the World Council of Churches and even the pope. Others included a Who's Who of charismatic theologians, educators, and evangelists.

8

DELIVERANCE!

We arrived at Christ Church, and the congregation was singing already, even though the service had not officially begun. This was normal procedure. Someone would begin singing spontaneously, and before long, others joined in. Most lifted their hands toward heaven and praised God *out loud*! Christ Church was an exciting place, and the people were full of life. It was contagious.

The minister eventually introduced Dennis Bennett, the guest speaker, and said we were in for a treat. Bennett, an Episcopal priest, was catapulted into national fame in 1960 when *Time* ran an article on him.[1] He had since become known as "the father of the modern charismatic movement."

The soft-spoken Bennett came to the platform and told how he was baptized in the Holy Spirit and spoke in unknown tongues on April 3, 1960, while serving as rector of the thriving St. Mark's Episcopal Church in Van Nuys, California. Before long, some of his parishioners had a similar experience. Some congregants, however, voiced concern over the emotional outbursts in their traditional church and asked their bishop to intervene. He acquiesced and moved Bennett

1. "Speaking in Tongues," *Time* 76, no. 7 (August 15, 1960).

to St. Luke's Episcopal, a small church in Seattle. The new appointment was meant to be a demotion and punishment for rocking the denominational boat. When word spread about Bennett's experience and his subsequent reassignment, reporters from *Time, Newsweek, People*, and other publications camped out on his doorstep. Wire services soon picked up the story, and overnight, the winsome and dry-witted Bennett was being invited to give radio and television interviews.

Most historians of American Christianity mark the birth of the charismatic movement (i.e., the entrance of Pentecostalism into the mainline churches) to Bennett's experience in 1960. As a result, he became the unofficial spokesperson for the burgeoning movement. Three years later, he chronicled his spiritual journey in the book *Nine O'Clock in the Morning*, which became an instant best seller.[2]

I sat transfixed and held on to Bennett's every word, wondering if my recent experience was similar to a baptism in the Holy Spirit. I didn't speak in tongues, but I was totally enveloped in God's Spirit.

On Wednesday, we returned. Bennett announced, "Tonight, I want to speak on the dangers of the occult and psychic phenomena."

Dangers? What's he talking about? There is nothing wrong with psychic activities. They are from God!

Dennis Bennett disagreed and made a bold claim: psychic gifts are satanic counterfeits of God-given gifts. He spoke of the recent influx of counterfeit tennis shoes that had come into the United States: "They bear the name *Converse* and *Nike* but are cheap imitations. Unless you are able to recognize the real from the fake, you may become a victim of consumer fraud. In the same way, Satan passes off his counterfeits as genuine God-given gifts. We must be on guard," he warned, because "Satan disguises himself as an angel of light," and "his ministers also disguise themselves as ministers of righteousness" (2 Cor. 11:14–15).[3]

---

2. Dennis Bennett, *Nine O'Clock in the Morning* (Plainfield, NJ: Logos, 1970).
3. All verses taken from the New Revised Standard Version, unless otherwise indicated.

Bennett named some of these counterfeits: psychic healing, dream analysis, spiritualism, automatic writing, astrology, fortune-telling, Ouija boards, and transcendental meditation. He referenced Hebrew and Christian Scriptures to support his argument and quoted a dozen or so passages from the Bible.[4]

He then declared, "God will not tolerate us seeking guidance through occult means." King Saul's visit to a trance medium was an example of such disobedience and the subsequent punishment: "Saul died for his unfaithfulness; he was unfaithful to the LORD in that he did not keep the command of the LORD; moreover, he had consulted a medium, seeking guidance" (1 Chron. 10:13). Bennett also told of a fortune-teller who lost her power when Saint Paul cast out a "spirit of divination" (Acts 16:16–18). On another occasion Paul's converts in Ephesus gathered all their occult paraphernalia and books and burned them as an act of public repentance (Acts 19:19–20).

Father Bennett said we are living in the "last days," as Jesus predicted, when many "false prophets will arise and perform great signs and wonders, so as to lead astray, if possible, even the elect" (Matt. 24:22–25 ESV).

From my time at the Baltimore School of the Bible, I knew the Scriptures were the Word of God, so hearing Dennis Bennett read these unfamiliar verses and expounding on them hit me like a ton of bricks! I was guilty of the very activities that the Bible condemned — seeking guidance from the dead and believing psychic manifestations were from God! I was in danger of judgment!

Bennett concluded his talk with an invitation: "When you become involved in psychic activities, you open the door for demonic oppression. But here is the good news — tonight, Christ can set you free."

He then called us to respond. "Please come forward, kneel at this altar rail, and ask God to deliver you from occult bondage. I will be here to pray with you."

---

4. Lev. 19:31; 20:6; Deut. 4:19; 17:2–5, 18:9–12; 2 Kings 21:3, 51; 1 Chron. 10:13; Isa. 47:10–14; Jer. 8:1–2; 10:2; 27:9–10; Dan. 2:1–4; 4:7; 5:7–9; Zeph. 1:5; Job 31:26–28; Ezek. 13:3; Acts 8:22; 16:16–18; Gal. 5:19–20; Rev. 21:7.

As soon as the music began, I was the first person to get up and walk forward. Father Bennett gently laid his hands on my head and quietly prayed. When I opened my eyes, I felt like an invisible weight was lifted from my shoulders. I was set free.

My friends rejoiced with me, and we talked on the way back to campus and late into the night.

What a week it had been — both reconciled to God and released from demonic darkness!

Lying in bed that night, I knew I must contact Ted Swager and warn him of the dangers of spiritualism before it was too late. *I will write to him tomorrow and tell him what happened to me.*

9

A Demon behind Every Bush

My entire perspective on psychic phenomena changed in a single night. I soon discovered there was a vast body of literature
written by charismatic and evangelical Christians who looked askance
at occult activities.[1] One book, *The Haunting of Bishop Pike*, by Merrill F. Unger, focused specifically on spiritualism.[2] Unger was an Old
Testament scholar with two earned doctorates from Johns Hopkins
University and Dallas Theological Seminary, respectively.[3] In his book
he argued that Bishop Pike had not contacted his dead son but was deceived by an evil spirit speaking through the voice of Arthur Ford.

If Dennis Bennett and Merrill Unger were correct (and I was now
convinced they were), I needed to warn Ted Swager. So, I wrote a
lengthy letter telling him about my dorm-room experience after hear-

1. Two of the more popular charismatic titles were Hobart E. Freeman,
Angels of Light? How to Be Set Free from Occult Oppression and Bondage (Plainfield,
NJ: Logos, 1971), and Raphael Gasson, *The Challenging Counterfeit: An Exposé
of Psychic Phenomena* (Plainfield, NJ: Logos, 1969).

2. Merrill F. Unger, *The Haunting of Bishop Pike: A Christian View of the Other
Side* (Wheaton, IL: Tyndale House, 1971).

3. At Hopkins Unger studied under William F. Albright, considered the
greatest archaeologist of his day.

ing Ed Bauman's lecture (I knew the mention of Bauman would grab Ted's attention). I shared my recent visit to Christ Church and hearing Dennis Bennett speak on the difference between real and counterfeit spiritual gifts. I included several biblical references and encouraged Ted to read them and to break with spiritualism.

I knew this letter might end our friendship but believed Ted's eternal destiny was at stake. I had to take the risk.

That weekend I traveled back to Baltimore and told my parents about my life-changing week. They did not understand how one minute I enthusiastically promoted psychic phenomena and the next I labeled it demonic. My mother and I argued over the issue.

On Sunday, I stood in the pulpit and shared my story with my congregation. They were very kind and forgiving. For the remainder of the semester, I basked in the light of my newfound faith. Everything in the world looked brighter.

✦

In May 1972, I completed the requirements for the master of divinity degree and received an appointment to serve as full-time pastor of a country church about thirty miles northwest of Baltimore.

Since my radical conversion, my preaching took on new life. I wanted my church members to know Jesus the way I did. So, I preached the gospel weekly and called for my congregants to repent and surrender to Jesus as Lord. Within weeks, the church began to grow and experience a fresh spiritual vitality.

I included a special time for prayer in the order of worship, called "The Ministry of Faith," and invited people forward for healing. Many responded. Two instances are worth a mention.

Larry Taylor, a husband and father, was a hardworking, quiet, "keep-to-yourself" type of person. I knew he had a serious problem when he stepped forward. Larry told me that doctors found a tumor the size of a grapefruit in his abdomen. The bulge was actually visible to the eye. He was scheduled for surgery the following Wednesday. We prayed together, and when he visited the oncologist that week, the tumor was gone! The following Sunday he showed me his flat belly and we rejoiced.

On another occasion, Jimmy Flater called and asked me to visit his daughter Madge, a single mother of two preteen boys, who was in the hospital for a hysterectomy. The diagnosis was ovarian cancer. When I prayed for her, I sensed that God had touched her body. Not wanting to seem presumptuous, I said nothing, but asked Jimmy to make sure the doctor examined her one more time before surgery. The phone rang early the next morning. Jimmy was on the other end and so choked up he could hardly speak. "We're bringing Madge home within the hour," he said. "They couldn't find any cancer."

In a bold move, I brought John and Patti Secret on staff to lead our music. John, one of my classmates, was in his last year at seminary. From a traditional Pentecostal background, the Secrets were unashamed of showing emotion, raising their hands, and saying a hearty "Praise the Lord." They were wonderful singers and transformed our worship.

The church grew numerically and appeared to be healthy. However, a few oldline families were up in arms and called a "secret" meeting (no pun intended). They had two main complaints. First, they disliked the new style of worship, which they called "a three-ring circus." Second, they were afraid that new members might soon take over "their" church. They contacted the district superintendent and demanded my transfer (shades of Dennis Bennett!). Not willing to be bullied, he refused. In fact, he reappointed me for another year!

The dissenters remained hostile, withheld their tithes, and sought to make my life miserable.[4] In September 1973, I resigned and took a position as executive director of Hampstead Youth for Christ (HYFC), a parachurch organization that sponsored monthly rallies to reach teenagers for Christ. HYFC was in debt; so, I devoted my first months to raising funds. Once things were financially solvent, I turned my attention to bolstering evangelism. I contacted speakers, built a mailing list, reached out to church youth groups, advertised, and trained

---

4. But all was not a loss. I met my future wife at the church, and we have been happily married ever since.

counselors. Our first rally speaker was Nicky Cruz, the famed New York gang member turned evangelist and subject of the best-selling book *The Cross and the Switchblade*.[5] Because of his name recognition and our hard work, over 1,200 teens packed the North Carroll High School gymnasium, and more than 50 responded to the gospel invitation. Each month we repeated the pattern.

One spring afternoon in 1974, I answered my office phone and heard a familiar voice on the other end: "Al, this is Ted Swager. Praise God, I've been delivered!"

I couldn't believe my ears. *Was Ted pulling my leg or sincere?*

Ted assured me that he had turned his back on mediumship and walked away from his beautiful Spiritual Center on the shores of the Chesapeake Bay. He said he wanted to meet and fill me in on the details.

Ted and Lois drove up from southern Maryland, and we met for lunch at a local Holiday Inn. As soon as I spotted them getting out of their car and walking toward me, I knew something had changed. They both looked happy and carefree, with a noticeable bounce in their steps. Ted began talking immediately. I don't think he ever ate his lunch. He told me that after he read my multipage epistle, he was angry. But after a time of reflection, he began to reassess his ministry and didn't like what he saw. The majority of his clients were curiosity seekers with little interest in serving God. Disconcerted over the perceived shallowness of their ministry, Ted and Lois prayed for guidance. They decided to visit the midweek service of a small Pentecostal church in their area, hoping that God might speak to them. Ted confided, "In my days as a respectable Methodist minister, I would have never been caught dead in a place like that."

When the pastor invited people to the altar for prayer, they went forward. Their prayer was simple: "Give us a sign. If people don't want Jesus, drive them away."

Smiling, Ted said, "Al, calls came in almost immediately canceling previously scheduled readings. With no readings for three weeks, income dried up fast."

---

5. David Wilkerson with John Sherrill and Elizabeth Sherrill, *The Cross and the Switchblade* (New York: Bernard Geis Associates, 1963).

Ted and Lois returned to the small church to pray again and seek God's mind about their future. On this occasion, as they knelt at the front, Ted began to "speak in tongues" and Lois felt a mysterious force strike her in the small of the back. When she stood, she realized that a painful spinal problem she had had for years was gone. It never returned.

Ted contacted his extensive client list to inform them that he would no longer be accepting appointments for readings and that he was renouncing the occult. With little income, they couldn't pay the mortgage on the Spiritual Center, and they moved out of their spacious home into a cramped rental property in Edgewood, Maryland. Ted began painting houses for a living.

As I looked around the hotel restaurant, I imagined what the other diners would think if they overheard our conversation.

I interrupted Ted: "Everyone should hear your story. You must get the word out!"

Ted hemmed and hawed and finally confessed, "I have to keep painting just to feed my family."

"Well, you can come and tell your story at a Youth for Christ rally."

His eyes lit up. "Really?"

"Yes. Let's set a date."

Three months later Ted spoke to a large crowd at North Carroll High School. I recorded his testimony and sent a copy to Bob Whittaker, the owner of a Christian publishing house. As a result, they offered Ted a book contract and assigned a ghostwriter to tell his story.[6]

Launching Out on My Own

As the executive director of HYFC I was responsible for publicity, raising funds, chairing board meetings, contacting potential speakers, and organizing rallies. Administration was not my strong suit. I wanted to spend more time in ministry, and in 1975 I formed Streett Meetings,

---

6. From the start, Ted and the ghostwriter locked horns over theology and how the book should be written. As a result, Ted backed out of the contract, and the book never got written.

Inc. (SMI), a 501(c) 3 nonprofit organization, which allowed me to preach and teach full time.

I sent scores of letters to local church ministers and offered to fill their pulpits or conduct weeklong evangelistic meetings. Many knew me from HYFC and responded positively. I spoke in Methodist, Lutheran, Episcopal, Presbyterian, Brethren, Pentecostal, Church of God, and independent churches throughout the region. Hundreds of people over the next eight years dedicated their lives to Christ.

In addition, I taught an SMI-sponsored evening Bible class each week at the local high school with thirty or so regular attendees. Teaching became my first love, and I hoped that one day I might be able to teach at a Bible college or seminary.

Because of my previous psychic involvement, I felt obligated to warn people of its dangers. I began researching and collecting data on numerous cults, sects, and occult practices until I amassed one of the largest collections of countercult materials in America.

On November 18, 1978, when the Jonestown massacre was first reported, Americans sat glued to their TV sets as pictures scrolled across their screens showing 909 lifeless bodies strewn on the grounds of a makeshift worship center.[7] Jim Jones, a self-proclaimed prophet and miracle man, persuaded the faithful members of the Peoples Temple to drink Kool-Aid laced with poison. Every major media outlet covered the story.

WTOW, a local Christian radio station, contacted me for my opinion and insights on the mass suicide/murder. I had collected information on Jim Jones for three years. With file in hand, I hopped into my car and drove to the studio. The manager interviewed me for an hour and opened the phone lines. The small five-thousand-watt radio station got the highest ratings in the market during that time slot, beating out stations ten times its size.

This opened the door for me to do a weekly show. Drawing on my vast amount of information, I devoted each program to a different cult group

---

7. It was the highest single-day death toll in American history until September 11, 2001.

or psychic practice. The broadcast grew in popularity and expanded to more than a dozen stations in New York, New Jersey, Tennessee, Florida, California, Indiana, Pennsylvania, Maryland, Ohio, and several Caribbean islands. To complement the show, I wrote a monthly magazine-style newsletter that included a pullout on a cult group or occult activity that could be placed in a three-ring binder for future reference.

Realizing the power of the printed word, I wrote three books,[8] which SMI published and distributed throughout the United States. I also submitted many articles to magazines and journals.

Whenever I shared my testimony and deliverance from the occult, the message received a positive response. As a result, the Full Gospel Business Men's Fellowship International (FGBMFI) invited me to speak at chapter meetings throughout the state. Most were held in restaurants or hotel ballrooms and included dinner, lively music, a speaker, and an invitation. People praised God openly, and the meetings pulsated with energy.

Full Gospel Business Men's Fellowship International

The founder, Demos Shakarian, was the firstborn son of parents who escaped the Armenian genocide in 1905 and fled to America, where they settled in Los Angeles. A year later, they were converted in the historic Azusa Street revival. Demos worked alongside his father on the family dairy farm, which prospered and eventually became one of the largest privately owned dairies in the world. Upon his father's death, Demos used his inheritance for evangelism. In 1956, he founded the FGBMFI, whose sole mission was to reach businessmen for Christ. Christian executives were encouraged to invite colleagues to have dinner at a nice restaurant and hear a speaker.

By 1975, the FGBMFI had grown to 1,650 chapters worldwide, and over 500,000 men attended monthly meetings. Each time I spoke to a

---

8. Alan Streett, *The Occult: Its Demonic Nature* (Finksburg, MD: SMI, 1975); *The Invaders: A Biblical Study of UFO's* (Finksburg, MD: SMI, 1975); and *In High Places: A Study of Occult and Government* (Finksburg, MD: SMI, 1977).

group, I told about my occult involvement, encounter with God, and being set free when Dennis Bennett laid hands on me. I always closed with an appeal. On one such occasion, a somewhat nervous, nattily dressed gentleman with pure white hair stepped forward.

Syd Smith was a retired naval officer and UFO enthusiast, and as a young career officer serving in Alaska with the Nike Missile Battalion (a highly secretive defense group that protects America from attack), he heard rumors of UFO sightings. Syd decided to investigate and on several occasions questioned the ship's radar men who had made the reports. They confirmed tracking unidentified objects on their screens, which raised an immediate "red alert."

After he retired, Syd, who came from a family of scientists, became a serious student of ufology. The Aerial Phenomena Research Organization, the oldest UFO research group in America, certified Syd as an accredited investigator. As his interests in psychic phenomena broadened, he joined the Spiritual Frontiers Fellowship and attended meetings regularly. Then in 1975, a friend invited him to an FGBMFI dinner at the Hecht Company restaurant in Towson, Maryland, where I was guest speaker. Once Syd realized we had moved in similar circles, he listened intently to my testimony. As a result, he renounced his involvement in the occult and made a commitment to Christ. We became lifelong friends.

During the early 1970s, America was undergoing an occult explosion as millions explored Eastern mysticism in its many forms. The Ouija board outsold Monopoly for the first time since its creation in 1903. Others turned to mind-expanding drugs in search of God. As a result, my countercult ministry grew, and more speaking engagements came my way. Then in the spring of 1978, I received a surprise note from Ted Swager.

10

A Tragic Setback

My heart sank when I checked my mailbox and discovered a handwritten postcard: "Reverend Ted Swager is now available to provide trance readings, dream interpretation, and counseling." It included Ted's new Maryland address and phone number.

Ted was at it again!

Saddened by the news, I immediately called Dr. Pyke, my old friend and professor. He, too, had received a similar announcement. After a long discussion, we decided to hold an "intervention" to save Ted from making a big mistake and ruining his Christian testimony. We asked Ted if he would meet with us on the campus of Wesley Theological Seminary, saying we wanted to learn more about this new venture and to understand his reason for returning to spiritualism. He agreed.

We gathered on a Wednesday afternoon in an empty classroom. From the start of the meeting our conversation was awkward and uncomfortable. I was certain I could feel an evil presence and that we were fighting satanic forces in a battle for Ted's soul!

When we asked Ted to tell us why he was returning to spiritualism, he replied, "I am completely disillusioned with the church. No denomination will support me as a full-time evangelist." We could hear the disappointment in his voice.

"So," he continued, "I launched out on my own. I wanted to tell my story and preach against the occult. I even asked God to give me the gift of healing. After all, if the devil gave me supernormal powers when I was a trance medium, why shouldn't God do the same now that I was saved? But the miracles never came and the speaking engagements were few and far between."

In order to support his family, Ted took a job as a car salesman. As he became more discouraged, he started to regret closing down the Spiritual Center. This led to a long period of introspection and a re-evaluation of the nature of spiritualism and psychic gifts. Drawing on the writings of philosopher William James and psychotherapist Carl Jung, Ted concluded that the information he received while in trance came from his subconscious mind and not from demons or the spirits of the dead.

Ted then dropped the bomb: "Last month, I placed myself into a trance for the first time in years," he said, then added, "it felt good and I knew everything was going to be okay."

Dr. Pyke and I were floored.

"Ted, how do you *know* these words were not from the devil?"

"Because they were God honoring," he quickly replied.

"But Ted, the Bible says, 'Satan disguises himself as an angel of light' and 'his ministers also disguise themselves as ministers of righteousness'" (2 Cor. 11:14–15).

No matter what we said or how strongly we pleaded with him to reconsider his decision, he did not listen. He had made up his mind; so, Dr. Pyke prayed and the meeting ended.

I lost contact with Ted but later heard he had moved to Memphis, Tennessee, to become religious and parapsychological consultant for the Counseling and Education Center at the Lakeside Psychiatric Hospital.[1] While there he also reestablished his relationship with the United Methodist Church and pastored local churches in the area.

---

1. I wondered how Ted landed such a position. Then I came across an old SFF newsletter: vol. 4, no. 1 (January 1970), which mentioned that Ted gave

Over the next decade, I devoted my energies to sounding the alarm against demonic deception. While I did not believe demons lurked behind *every* bush, I was pretty sure they had infiltrated every aberrant religious group imaginable.

I continued speaking at FGBMFI events but noticed a subtle change in their meetings. Teaching and preaching took a back seat to emotional outbursts and wild manifestations, ranging from bizarre words of prophecy that defied common sense to people jerking or falling onto the floor "under the power of the Spirit." From my study of the Scriptures, I became concerned that the charismatic movement as a whole had devolved into a cult of personalities, self-promotion, and out-of-control displays of the flesh.

I listened regularly on the radio to conservative Bible teachers who preached verse-by-verse through the Scriptures and read theology books written by scholars from evangelical seminaries. The last time I spoke at a charismatic gathering, the host approached me afterward and said, "You sound more like a Baptist than one of us." I agreed.

I was more at home in evangelical churches, that is, ones that were theologically sound and held similar beliefs as those taught at the Baltimore School of the Bible. I stopped speaking for charismatic churches and FGBMFI.

Sensing a need for more biblical education, I began searching for a doctoral program and spotted an advertisement in *Christianity Today* for California Graduate School of Theology (Glendale, California), an independent/nondenominational school.[2]

Besides its main campus, the school operated extensions throughout the United States and Korea. Their innovative approach to education enabled busy pastors to travel once a month to a regional

---

a three-day series of lectures in Memphis, followed by a weeklong workshop on psychic phenomena. Evidently he had made some important connections.

2. California Graduate School of Theology is now a graduate school of Haven University (Garden Grove, CA).

site and work on their graduate degrees. I was accepted into the program in 1978, and for three years drove from my home in Baltimore to the New York extension for classes. I spent another year writing my dissertation: "The Public Invitation: Its History, Theology, and Practicability."[3]

In May 1982, I walked across the stage at the Glendale campus and received my PhD diploma.

Dr. Paige Patterson, president of Criswell College (Dallas, Texas), had read a copy of my dissertation and, as a result, invited me to speak to the student body at a specially called chapel service. After my lecture, he took me to lunch and offered me a position as professor of New Testament and evangelism. It was a dream come true!

Criswell College is located in the buckle of the Bible Belt. Established in 1972 by W. A. Criswell, the fiery orator and fighting fundamentalist pastor of First Baptist Church, Dallas, the college was at the forefront of the conservative resurgence (the battle for biblical inerrancy) in the Southern Baptist Convention. Believing America's largest denomination and its six seminaries were turning liberal, Criswell founded the Criswell Bible Institute (very similar to the Baltimore School of the Bible) to combat the progressive trend and to raise up a new generation of preachers who stood for the old-time religion.

By the time of my hiring, the school had morphed into a Bible college and graduate school of theology. Under the leadership of Patterson, it played a significant role in turning the Convention in a more conservative direction. Patterson believed I could both preach and staunchly defend the faith against all forms of doctrinal deviation. He called me "the Cult Buster" and promised to find a slot on KCBI-FM, the 100,000-watt college-owned and -operated radio station.

On January 3, 1983, my family arrived in Dallas. I instantly had a larger platform and wider audience than ever before. As a college

---

3. It would later be published under the title *The Effective Invitation* (Old Tappan, NJ: Revell, 1984).

professor, people respected me and looked to me for answers. I taught
New Testament, evangelism, apologetics, and my hallmark course,
"The Theology of Cults."

These were exciting but turbulent times.[4]

4. Within a few months of arriving in Dallas I received a copy of the *Capital*
(May 12, 1983), the major newspaper out of Annapolis, MD, that announced
the public auction of the Spiritual Center for Healing, Counseling, and Parapsychology. It read in all caps: "SUBSTITUTE TRUSTEES SALE OF VALUABLE
WATERFRONT PROPERTY." Following the latitudinal and longitudinal location, the property was described as "a brick, colonial dwelling" improved with
"tennis courts, swimming pool, and other amenities" that sits on "Herring Bay,
an arm of the Chesapeake Bay." To emphasize its value, the notice added, "It is
one of the most desirable waterfront properties in the State of Maryland." I was
sickened as I reflected on Ted Swager's ill-fated and confused life as a spiritualist. The splendid property that he once hoped would serve as an international
headquarters for his psychic exploits was now being sold at auction from the
steps of the courthouse.

PART 3

II

Magic and the Witch Doctor

My son Daniel had many different hobbies in his young life, including stamp collecting, karate, BMX biking, collecting football cards, Commodore computers, and magic. He checked out several books on magic and magicians from the public library. His enthusiasm was contagious, and before long I took up the hobby. Daniel's interest eventually waned, and he moved on to another hobby. But I was hooked!

My First Visit to a Magic Shop

When I first visited a magic shop, I was like a duck out of water. I wandered around aimlessly among the displays of gag tricks like whoopie cushions and exploding cigarettes. The owner, who happened to be the only salesperson, sized me up immediately and knew I was a novice. Professional magicians know that the "good stuff" is hidden out of sight. At an opportune time, the owner stepped from behind the counter, introduced herself as Madeline, and asked if I would like to see a trick. I nodded, and she reached into a drawer and retrieved a two-by-two-inch red plastic square a half-inch thick. She took my hand, turned it palm down, and began to spin a tale: "Magicians throughout the ages have attempted to change base metals into gold. It is rumored that long ago one discovered the secret, but he took it with him to the grave. Ever since, magicians have tried to rediscover his secret, but with little success."

With a slight smile and a twinkle in her eyes, Madeline laid a shiny Lincoln penny on the back of my hand and placed the small red block on top of it. After mumbling a few archaic words, she lifted the block and the penny was transformed into a brilliant silver dime!

"Alchemy!" she declared with a hint of surprise. "Imagine if we could still change copper into *gold*!"

I was dumbfounded and excited.

Recognizing a potential sale, Madeline pushed to close the deal: "If you buy this trick, I will show you how it is done."

I plopped $7.95 onto the counter, and she performed the trick slowly and explained it step-by-step. It was so simple and obvious! How did I miss it? I still perform this trick for my grandchildren, and it's as much fun doing it now as it was three decades ago.

Feeling more comfortable, I asked her to recommend a good book on magic.

Handing me *Tarbell's Course in Magic*, volume 1, she said, "This should fit the bill. It covers all the basics. Magicians have used it for over a half century."

THE TARBELL COURSE IN MAGIC

As soon as I got home I began to read. The introduction gave a brief history of the Tarbell Course, which originated in 1911 as a five-year mail-order course in magic. Each month a new lesson was sent to subscribers.[1] One statement caught my eye. "Students enrolled not only

---

1. The lessons were eventually compiled and converted into five hardback books. In 1941, three more volumes were added. To this day, the Tarbell Course eight-volume set remains the gold standard for those wishing to obtain a complete education in magic.

from every country of the world, but from islands and places I had never heard of. Even Witch Doctors of Bali and Africa were enrolled. The sending of lessons and apparatus to Witch Doctors is a story all by itself. Lessons were crumpled up amongst packing paper and sent in a box containing some sort of trinket. Magical apparatus was carefully disguised and sent as something else."[2]

Felix Shay, a professional magician of yesteryear, reported traveling in Africa where he witnessed a witch doctor perform miracles that he recognized immediately as the same tricks found in the Tarbell Course. In India he had a similar experience with a Hindu fakir. Upon investigating, he discovered that both were subscribers to the monthly Tarbell lessons.[3]

Although these mystery men claimed to possess special powers, they actually performed magic tricks.

My imagination ran wild. Was it possible that some psychics do the same thing? I decided to investigate and soon discovered that magic as a form of entertainment is a relatively recent phenomenon, dating back only a few hundred years. Prior to that, people believed wonder-workers possessed *real* power to cast spells, remove curses, cure diseases, control weather and crops, and call fire down from heaven. Known variously as shamans, medicine men, witches, wizards, magi, alchemists, and astrologers, they often chanted, danced, drew circles around themselves, concocted potions, or repeated secret incantations to achieve "supernatural" results. Most invoked the name of a deity or called on spirits for help. They were essential to the welfare of their respective community, tribe, or nation.

THE DISCOVERIE OF WITCHCRAFT

With the expansion of Christianity in the West, the church took a dim view of shamanism and labeled it demonic in origin. During the

---

2. Harlan Tarbell, *Tarbell Course in Magic* (Brooklyn, NY: D. Robbins, 1971), xiv.

3. Tarbell, *Tarbell Course in Magic*, xiv.

mid- to late sixteenth century, Catholic and Protestant churches, along with the British monarchy, waged war against occultism. The Witchcraft Act (1563) authorized the death penalty for those convicted of sorcery. Sir Reginald Scot (1538–1599), an educated and enlightened gentleman-farmer, who later became a magistrate in Kent, England, opposed the act, knowing that the witches were actually devious charlatans. In an effort to stop unwarranted prosecutions, he wrote *The Discoverie of Witchcraft* (1584), in which he exposed the tricks that witches and other soothsayers used (e.g., sleight of hand, misdirection, and illusions) to accomplish their feats. *Discoverie* was the first major book in the English language to reveal the secrets of magic.

Scot, who later became a member of Parliament in 1588, failed in his attempt. Legislators and judges, fearful of offending the ecclesiastic authorities, were unpersuaded. To make matters worse, the witches themselves refused to admit their chicanery. When King James VI succeeded Queen Elizabeth (1603), he ordered all copies of Scot's book removed from circulation and burned in public view, calling it "damnable" and saying it opposed the official stance of the church.[4]

In time, Scot's thesis was proved to be true, and other enlightened writers wrote similar volumes exposing the tricks of the shaman's trade.[5]

André Kole (1932–2022) was one of the most respected inventors of magic tricks and illusions.[6] Professional magicians such as David Copperfield and David Blaine have performed Kole's illusions on nationwide television and have fooled millions. In his book *From Illusion to Reality*, Kole recounts his travels around the world.[7] He tells how he

4. At least one copy of Scot's book survived. It has since been reprinted and the Olde English updated. Reginald Scot, *The Discoverie of Witchcraft* (New York: Dover, 1972).

5. Despite the facts, most churches — even today — characterize psychic phenomena as manifestations of demonic power, when they may be nothing more than demonstrations of legerdemain.

6. Kole, an evangelical Christian, also worked for Campus Crusade for Christ.

7. André Kole and Al Janssen, *From Illusion to Reality* (San Bernardino, CA: Here's Life, 1984).

observed firsthand Indian gurus and African witch doctors perform seemingly supernatural feats. One supposedly raised a man from the dead. Another produced lost objects out of thin air. When Kole privately confronted the village enchanters and identified himself as a professional magician, they knew they had been caught and quickly confessed their trickery (shades of Tarbell!). However, they all claimed pure motives and said they just wanted to help people. One witch doctor even had the audacity to ask Kole to teach him a few new tricks!

Throughout the centuries shamans have closely guarded their secrets, passing down their hidden knowledge to only their most trusted pupils. It was imperative their modus operandi never be revealed, lest they *lose face* and the masses *lose faith*. This tradition continues in remote societies not touched by the Enlightenment, where villagers view the tribal shaman as a wonder-worker.

But what about modern civilizations, where education and science rule the day? Are we any different from ancient or backward cultures? After all, thousands turn to psychics for paranormal insight to make decisions regarding health, business, and affairs of the heart. Others believe certain individuals possess healing virtue emanating from their fingertips, just as I once did with Olga Worrall.

Who are these specially endowed persons? Are they agents of Satan, as Dennis Bennett believed, or shamanistic fakers like André Kole confronted?

This question drove me to continue my research and led to my next major discovery — a specialized branch of magic known as *mentalism*.

MENTALISM

In our day and age, everyone knows that professional magicians use tricks to entertain audiences. We do not believe a performer actually saws a person in half or that a little red cube can change a penny into a dime. Magicians are masters of sleight of hand and misdirection, or they use props to accomplish their illusionary marvels. If stage magicians ever claimed their wonders were real, who would take them seriously?

Mentalism, however, is a whole different ball of wax. It is magic of the mind. The performer, known as a mentalist, possesses an uncanny ability to read thoughts, predict the future, and bend a steel rod by mind power, or so it seems. These "psychic" feats take years of study and practice to master.

Joseph Dunninger (1892–1975) was the preeminent mentalist of the late 1940s and '50s. Multitudes listened to his weekly radio show as he told people where to find lost objects and offered them advice about the future. The distance between Dunninger and his radio audience did not hinder his ability as a seer. When he later transitioned to television, his audience grew even larger. Most people believed Dunninger was a genuine psychic. He never affirmed or denied it but let the audience decide for themselves. One of his favorite sayings was "To those who believe, no explanation is necessary. To those who don't believe, no explanation is possible."

From the 1960s to the 1980s, "the Amazing Kreskin" stepped into the national limelight. His appearance on popular talk shows guaranteed even larger audiences, and his demonstrations of ESP left viewers scratching their heads in amazement. Kreskin never claimed to be a psychic, but neither did he dissuade those who believed it to be true.[8]

Although they refused to admit it, both Dunninger and Kreskin were simply well-trained magicians who played the part of psychics.

Unethical mentalists, however, aggressively promote themselves as *real* psychics.[9]

8. Kreskin was one of only a few mentalists who mastered the art of muscle reading, which enabled him to perform seemingly telepathic feats. At the close of each show, he asked a committee to hide his paycheck in the theater and then he departed. Upon returning, Kreskin selected a volunteer, held her hand, and began to search. As the audience members watched with bated breath, the volunteer unintentionally and subconsciously led Kreskin to the secret spot. If he did not find the paycheck, he did not get paid! Only once did he fail.

9. In 1978, the Psychic Entertainers Association was formed to promote ethical standards and practices for psychic entertainers. Over two hundred of the world's top mentalists are members.

Uri Geller is an example of one who claimed to have special powers. He gained international fame for his ability to bend forks, spoons, and knives through the power of his mind alone. He astonished viewers as they watched metal objects melt before their eyes. When asked how he did it, Geller responded, "I am not sure, except that I concentrate on an object and inwardly command it, *Bend! Bend!* And it does! I am as mystified as you." As Geller's reputation grew, a personality cult developed around him. It soon came crashing down when James Randi, himself a world-class magician and honest mentalist, exposed Geller as nothing more than a faker and revealed his methods.[10]

David Hoy (1930–1981), a Christian minister from Paducah, Kentucky, used stage magic as an evangelistic tool to spread the gospel. A graduate of the controversial Bob Jones University, he preached and performed his tricks in fundamentalist churches across America. In time, he left the ministry and became a professional mentalist, performing under the name Dr. Faust. He wrote three instructional books for magicians and invented several widely used tricks, including the classic Tossed Out Deck. In the early 1970s, however, Hoy started passing himself off as a "real" psychic, calling himself "the Paducah Prophet." His magician friends attempted to dissuade Hoy, but he scorned their advice. Touting himself as one of America's foremost authorities on ESP, he said he predicted that Jackie Kennedy would marry Aristotle Onassis, and that, after winning the California primary, Bobby Kennedy would face tragedy. In 1974, John Godwin penned Hoy's biography, *Super-Psychic: The Incredible Dr. Hoy*.[11] As his fame grew, Hoy wrote a syndicated column, carried in 350 newspapers. The gullible public held on to his every word.

When unethical mentalists claim to be bona fide psychics, the results can be disastrous as the unsuspecting public places its misguided faith in their powers.

10. James Randi, *The Truth about Uri Geller* (Amherst, NY: Prometheus, 1982).
11. John Godwin, *Super-Psychic: The Incredible Dr. Hoy* (New York: Pocket Books, 1974).

The blockbuster movie *Nightmare Alley* (2021), starring Bradley Cooper and based on the book by the same title, graphically drives home this point.[12] Stan Carlisle, a drifter, hooks up with a rundown carnival, where he meets Pete, a retired mentalist who teaches him the tricks of the trade but warns him never to use the knowledge unethically. Carlisle disregards the advice and launches out on his own, rising to stardom. But in the midst of growing success, he crosses the line and promises a wealthy client that he will conjure up the spirit of a dead loved one. The scam ends in tragedy and murder.

✦

I had to come to grips with the possibility that many psychics were actually mentalists gone wrong. This was a sobering thought, since for a dozen years I had brazenly accused all psychics of being demon possessed and agents of the devil. Now I was forced to reassess my position.

Dan Korem, an investigative reporter and world-class magician, helped me see that I had been "barking up the wrong tree." Korem used his knowledge of mentalism to expose psychic frauds. His TV documentary *Psychic Confession* chronicles his yearlong investigation of James Hydrick, whose paranormal demonstrations on *That's Incredible* led to notoriety and a cult-like following. Not suspecting that Korem was a professional magician, Hydrick allowed him to videotape his psychic exploits of mind power. At a strategic moment in the program, Korem replicates one of Hydrick's "psychic tricks." The bewildered Hydrick becomes agitated and angry. The documentary ends with Korem identifying himself and Hydrick confessing on camera that he is a psychic fraud.[13]

When I discovered that Korem lived in the greater Dallas area, I invited him to speak to my "Theology of the Cults" class at Criswell College. He graciously came to campus, gave an excellent lecture on psychic deception, and then did a few mentalism tricks. He wowed us all.

12. William L. Gresham, *Nightmare Alley* (New York: Signet, 1946).
13. Dan Korem, *Psychic Confession* (Dallas: Korem Productions, 1986).

In a private conversation, Korem told me he had never come across a psychic that was not a faker — no exceptions![14] They have simply learned the secrets of mentalism either by reading published materials or by observing mentalists at work.

To test Korem's thesis, I needed to learn the secrets of mentalism for myself. I made another trip to the magic store, and Madeline, the owner, suggested I read Corinda's *Thirteen Steps to Mentalism* (considered the Holy Grail of mentalism) and Ted Annemann's *Practical Mental Magic*.[15] The books included every kind of psychic trick imaginable and the step-by-step instructions to perform it. I read about spoon bending, mind reading, fortune-telling, clairvoyance, and more.[16] My imagination ran wild, and I now understood how unscrupulous scammers might use these methods in their quest for psychic legitimacy. During 1986, I spent any free time, aside from my classes and radio program, devouring the material until I became adept at mentalism myself.

14. Kole, *From Illusion to Reality*, 18, confirms Korem's conclusion: "When it comes to genuine psychic power, I have yet to investigate a demonstration that didn't prove to be the result of trickery."

15. Tony Corinda, *Thirteen Steps to Mentalism* (New York: Louis Tannen, 1968); Theodore Annemann, *Practical Mental Magic* (Brooklyn, NY: D. Robbins, 1944).

16. As I continued to delve into the nature of psychic phenomena, I discovered a subgenre of mentalism known as bizarre magic, which goes far beyond telepathy, precognition, and clairvoyance, and seeks to replicate black magic. To set the atmosphere, the bizarrist may utter an incantation, stick a needle in a voodoo doll, display the image of Baphomet, or invoke the spirits of the dead, which adds a level of mystique to the effect. Bizarre magic is an esoteric form of mentalism. Whenever bizarrists present themselves as real magicians of the black arts and human channels for dark spirits, danger lurks. An example of a bizarrist-gone-wrong is Aleister Crowley, who self-identified as the Beast of Revelation. He founded the Golden Dawn, a ceremonial cult whose followers offered sacrifices to the spirits, placed curses on enemies, and engaged in group orgies. In Roger Hutchinson, *Aleister Crowley: The Beast Demystified* (Edinburgh: Mainstream, 1998), 17, 214, Crowley is portrayed as a "charlatan" and "a poser who had come to believe his own poses."

I discovered the deuterocanonical book Bel and the Dragon, an apocryphal addition to the book of Daniel, which tells of Daniel's confrontation with the priests of Bel (a Persian god), who serve in the court of King Cyrus. When the king asks Daniel if he believes that Bel is a living god, Daniel says, "No, Bel is an idol made with hands." The priests, however, claim otherwise and present as evidence the fact that Bel consumes the daily meal and drink offering that is laid each night before the altar in the temple. Daniel sets out to prove them wrong. After the priests make the offering and leave, Daniel sneaks in and scatters ashes on the floor. The next morning the food is gone, but the priests' footprints are found in the ashes. They, not Bel, have eaten the sacrifice. Like modern-day charlatans, they proclaim a supernatural narrative, when in reality the so-called miracle has a natural explanation.[17]

TRICKS OF THE TRADE

Fraudulent psychics ply their trade in every big city and small town in America, often operating out of ramshackle residences in a seedy part of town with painted front-yard signs featuring a human hand, a deck of cards, or the head of a gypsy. Others, however, are of a different sort. They host television shows, give lectures at psychic conferences, and have the rich and famous among their clientele. They succeed because they are friendly, respectable, and good conversationalists, and their clients trust them.

Psychics cannot read minds or predict the future; otherwise, they would regularly win the lottery, "break the bank at Monte Carlo," and predict the yearly winners of the Kentucky Derby, Preakness, and Belmont Stakes. Nevertheless, they are good at convincing their gullible customers that they possess supernatural abilities and insight.

Clairvoyants succeed because they appear to deliver the goods! While they may not be able to predict a horse-race winner on demand, they seem to know about the past circumstances of their sitters and

17. Bel and the Dragon is part of the Apocrypha and located between the Hebrew and Christian Scriptures in some editions of the Bible.

information about their futures. To believers, these paranormal faculties are unmistakable. In reality, all psychics glean their information by natural means.

Method #1 — Cold Reading

The best psychics have mastered the art of cold reading.[18] This involves picking up cues from the unsuspecting sitters. Cold reading is a multilayered process that starts by tossing out a general observation such as "I see you are going through a somewhat difficult time." On the surface this may seem like psychic insight, but it is actually a *probe*. The psychic watches for a reaction. Does the sitter nod her head, twitch an eyebrow, or slightly frown? These involuntary movements are known as ideomotor responses or *tells* that inform the psychic how to proceed with the reading.[19] All responses are valuable. If given a frown, the psychic knows she has missed the mark. No problem. She simply takes her original statement ("I see you are going through a somewhat difficult time") and turns it into a warning: "You need to be on guard because I see a difficulty coming your way. It's right here in the cards."[20] Some sitters cooperate even more and offer *verbal* feedback to an initial probe: "Yes, I am worried that my youngest son is being badly influenced by his friends" or "I'm having trouble with my boss at work." The client has unknowingly served up valuable information on

18. Ian Rowland, *The Full Facts Book of Cold Reading* (London: Ian Rowland, 1998), is considered the best resource on cold reading ever written.

19. The ability of successful psychics to detect ideomotor responses is uncanny and intuitive. As they examine a person's palm, interpret a tarot card, or read tea leaves, they also spot facial cues and slight variations in breathing or body position. The best seers are indeed sensitives in the real sense of the word, for they perceive things that most of us miss. Some are so good at reading people it becomes almost second nature, and they start believing they possess psychic powers. In reality, their skills have a natural explanation.

20. Psychics use various props that give their readings an air of mystery and authenticity. Crystal balls, tarot cards, Ouija boards, tea leaves, *I Ching*, astrological charts, lifelines on the palm, and rune stones are just a few examples.

a silver platter. The psychic whispers to herself, *Thank you very much!* And proceeds to build on this bonus knowledge.

As an example, I remember my mother visiting Alma, the card reader, at the Palmer House restaurant in Baltimore. After a few niceties, Alma said, "You are a curious person who seeks answers about important matters."

Duh!

When my mother smiled, Alma continued, "I see someone in a uniform." This was a good guess or probe, especially since the Vietnam War was raging and my mother was of the age to have a son in the military. When my mother faintly furrowed her brow, Alma knew she was off base and started to change direction. But before she continued, my mother piped up, "My son Alan is going to be a minister. Maybe you saw him in a robe and clerical collar." This, of course, provided Alma with pertinent information.

"Yes, that's it," she replied, and then went on to talk about my future ministry and the good work I would do.

This was a "win-win" situation for both. My mother went away happy, and Alma was deemed a success. In reality, Alma was merely a good observer.

The best psychics have an innate ability to "read" people based on their clothes, hairstyle, hands, body language, jewelry, vocabulary, demeanor, age, the kind of car they drive, and even tattoos. To the astute observer, most people are an open book. Dan Korem's book *The Art of Profiling* is a classic on the subject, and has been used to train FBI agents, human resource directors, and others, in the techniques of reading people.[21]

Method #2 — Hot Reading

Most mind readers do not have the patience or ability to master cold-reading techniques; instead, they use a method known as hot reading.

21. Dan Korem, *The Art of Profiling: Reading People Right the First Time* (Richardson, TX: IFP, 1998).

This simply involves investigating clients prior to the date of the appointment, which allows the seer to give accurate readings based on the wealth of information gleaned from the Internet, Ancestry.com, and newspaper archives. These psychics cheat with their eyes wide open.

After studying mentalism, I concluded that most working psychics possess neither supernatural nor paranormal powers. I also resolved that my former thesis — most psychics are demon possessed — was misguided.

Scientists and Psychics

One thing still bothered me, however. Many respected scientists and academicians believe that certain individuals are endowed with psychic abilities. J. B. Rhine (1895–1980), who coined the term "ESP," and psychologist Karl Zener (1903–1964), the creator of the Zener cards, devoted years to examining the claims of psychics under test conditions. Using a set of twenty-five cards (each displaying one symbol: a circle, a cross, three wavy lines, a square, and a five-pointed star), the subject was asked to predict the symbol on each. The test was repeated at least fifty times. If the subject correctly guessed at a statistical rate higher than chance (one in five), the subject was deemed to have precognitive powers.

However, it was later discovered that the test conditions were flawed and open to fraud, thus rendering the results inconclusive.[22] When stricter tests were created that eliminated the possibility of cheating, the psychics were unable to outperform chance. Replication of test results is essential to scientific research.

Since scientists are unfamiliar with the craft of mentalism and the various means to produce miracles of the mind, they have a difficult time establishing protocols that guard against fraud.

As a teenager, Steve Shaw watched Uri Geller bend spoons and move objects. Rejecting Geller's outlandish explanation that he

---

22. Terence Hines, *Pseudoscience and the Paranormal* (Amherst, NY: Prometheus, 2003), 119–20.

achieved the results through mind power, Shaw set out to discover his surreptitious method. Before long Shaw mastered the art of spoon bending on demand.

When Geller mystified the scientists who tested him, Shaw realized these learned men were not adequately equipped to analyze the phenomenon. He knew he could fool them too. Shaw, along with mentalist James Randi, devised a devious plan. They contacted the McDonnell Laboratory for Psychic Research at Washington University (St. Louis) and asked if their professional investigators would test Steve Shaw, who had begun to exhibit increased paranormal powers. Over a two-year period, they put Shaw through a strenuous series of foolproof tests and concluded that he was the real deal, a legitimately gifted psychic.

To establish his bona fides Shaw submitted his telekinesis prowess to further scrutiny at the hands of Berthold E. Schwartz, MD, who reported the results in an article, "Taming the Poltergeist (Clinical Observations on Steve Shaw's Telekinesis)," which he submitted to a respected journal.[23] Schwartz concluded that Shaw had the uncanny ability to project mental images onto a roll of film.[24]

After the experiments were completed and the findings announced, Randi and Shaw stepped forward to reveal that they had deceived the scientists.[25] Shaw was not psychic at all, but had relied on tried and true mentalism tricks to dupe the researchers.

The embarrassed scientists learned a hard lesson. They were ill-prepared to spot deception because they were not privy to the methods used by mentalists — secrets closely guarded by the magic fraternity and rarely disclosed to outsiders.

23. Berthold E. Schwartz, "Taming the Poltergeist (Clinical Observations on Steve Shaw's Telekinesis)," *Journal of the American Society of Psychosomatic Dentistry and Medicine* 29, no. 4, supplement 6 (1982): 10.

24. Schwartz, "Taming the Poltergeist," 10.

25. James Randi, "The Project Alpha Experiment Part One," *Skeptical Inquirer* 7, no. 4 (1983): 24–33; "The Project Alpha Experiment Part Two," *Skeptical Inquirer* 8, no. 1 (Fall 1993): 36–45.

Shaw eventually went on to become a highly respected professional mentalist and entertainer and today performs under the stage name Banachek.

In 1986, Randi was named a recipient of a MacArthur Fellowship, also known as "the Genius Award," which included a $272,000 award for further research.

✦

Wanting my students to benefit from my research, I revised my lecture notes and added major sections on mentalism and psychic deception.

I continued to teach at Criswell College for two more years but was not happy with the direction of the school and resigned my position as a professor in the spring of 1988. I planted a new church in Dallas, and for the next ten years I preached through the books of the Bible and continued my investigation of psychic phenomena.

On Halloween eve of 1988, I was ready to put on display my newly acquired skills in mentalism. I rented a centrally located hotel ballroom and used my radio program and word-of-mouth to publicize and hype the event as the night when I would blow the lid off psychic deception.

Free tickets went fast. Over three hundred people filled the hall to hear my lecture and watch me perform. I read minds, described people's homes, called out unlisted phone numbers, named dead relatives, and revealed birthdays. I tossed in some humor to keep the atmosphere light. The audience sat amazed as I demonstrated and explained the mentalism principles and tricks employed by unscrupulous psychics to hoodwink the public.

I also gave the same performance during a Sunday morning church service in Southern California. The atmosphere was surreal because, at three o'clock that morning, an earthquake struck the area. I was jolted out of my bed and went immediately to the hotel parking lot, where other guests had gathered. It was an unsettling and restless night. As I stood behind the pulpit the next morning, the church crowd was very anxious and on edge. When I told them I had predicted the earthquake a week earlier (while still in Dallas), they looked at me like I was crazy. But when I showed them my personal diary where I had written down the prediction, their attitude changed. They didn't know what to make of my claims until I told them it was all a trick.

✦

In the back of my mind was the haunting suspicion that my friend Ted Swager and his mentor Arthur Ford were possibly fakers too. However, neither was a typical psychic. They didn't gaze into crystal balls, read tarot cards, or bend metal with their minds. They were spiritualists who served as channels between the living and the dead.

Was I wrong in suspecting Ted's legitimacy? To answer this question, I needed to take a good look at the history and inner workings of spiritualism.

I2

THE SPIRITUALISTS

To discover if Ted Swager was an impostor, I conducted an in-depth investigation into spiritualism. I was shocked by what I found! Spiritualism has always had its detractors who characterized mediums as swindlers and deceivers. If I discovered that Ted was likewise a con man playing the part of a trance medium, it would mean he had played me for a sucker for over thirty years. I dreaded to think about it; nevertheless, I forged ahead with my investigation.

Spiritualism in America can be traced to 1848 and Hydesville, New York, when fourteen-year-old Margaret and eleven-year-old Katie Fox heard strange rapping noises coming from the wall of their second-floor bedroom. Believing that a spirit entity might be trying to communicate with them, they asked their invisible guest to answer questions using a simple code of rapping. One rap meant *No*. Two raps, *Doubtful*. Three raps, *Yes*. Through this means, they discovered the spirit was that of Charles B. Rosna, a thirty-one-year-old peddler who had been murdered and secretly buried in the basement of their home many years earlier. The police later investigated and found a few bones on the property but no skeleton.

As word spread throughout the region, spectators flocked to the Fox residence hoping to hear the rapping for themselves. Rosna's spirit announced, however, that it would converse with the living only when the Fox sisters were present. Thus, Margaret and Katie became the first mediums in America.

Concerned for their daughters' welfare, Mr. and Mrs. Fox sought advice and counsel from local clergy but got diverse opinions. Some believed the spirit communication was divine in origin. Others said it came from the devil and was a threat to the girls' souls. In 1851, professors at the University of Buffalo concluded that the sisters produced the rappings by secretly cracking their knee joints under their long dresses. Margaret and Katie denied the accusations.

Their older sister Leah became their agent and arranged for them to demonstrate their prowess far and wide. The spirit of Charles Rosna followed. The girls achieved great fame at home and abroad. Margaret held séances for Queen Victoria, and Katie for the czar of Russia. Dr. Elisha Kane, the acclaimed Arctic explorer, took Margaret as his bride, and Horace Greeley, editor of the *New York Tribune*, paid for Katie's education. He and his wife regularly sought to communicate with their dead sons through Katie as the channel.

Spiritualism grew and evolved into a religious movement.[1] Before long, churches sprang up and clergy preached the gospel of Spiritualism — a belief that the soul is immortal and that the living can speak with the dead. By the outbreak of the Civil War, over two million Americans identified Spiritualism as their religion. Parents and spouses of soldiers killed in action sought proof of life after death. Spiritualism provided it.

Spiritualism, however, faced a major setback in October 1888 when both Fox sisters, now in their sixties — destitute and under the weight of guilt — confessed that they had used deceptive means from the start. They began to reveal and demonstrate their methods of trickery in public forums. Katie called spiritualism "the biggest humbug of the

---

1. When "spiritualism" is capitalized, it refers to the religion of Spiritualism. Written in lowercase, it speaks of contacting the dead through the means of a medium.

century." Margaret added, "I am here tonight as one of the founders of spiritualism to denounce it as an absolute falsehood."[2] While their confessions received significant coverage in New York newspapers, little attention was paid elsewhere. By this time, Spiritualism was unstoppable. On September 27, 1893, the National Spiritualist Association was formed and held its first delegate convention in Chicago to promote Spiritualism as a world religion.

✦

People often turn to trance mediums during time of war and plagues. Spiritualist activities, for instance, spiked during the Civil War, the Boer War, the two world wars, and the Vietnam War, as loved ones sought to contact soldiers killed in action. Mary Todd Lincoln even brought spiritualists into the White House in order to reach her son Willie, who died of typhoid fever in 1861.[3] The Spanish Flu of 1918 took forty million lives, and interest in spiritualism increased even more.

THINGS THAT GO BUMP IN THE DARK

At the close of the nineteenth century, *physical* mediums offered tangible evidence of life beyond the grave. Sitting at a séance table in a darkened room with a single flickering candle, they performed their chicanery and called on the spirits of the dead to manifest themselves in concrete ways. Oftentimes, faces appeared in the ether and hovered above the sitters; ectoplasm emanated from the orifices of the

2. Reuben B. Davenport, *The Deathblow to Spiritualism* (New York: G. W. Gillingham, 1888), 76.

3. In her book *Was Abraham Lincoln a Spiritualist?* Nettie Colburn Maynard claims she regularly visited the White House at the behest of Mary Todd Lincoln to conduct séances. The president occasionally attended these sessions. See N. C. Maynard, *Was Abraham Lincoln a Spiritualist?* (Philadelphia: Rufus C. Hartranft, 1891).

medium's body;[4] familiar apports (trinkets) fell down from the spirit world and landed in the sitters' laps; trumpets floated, bells rang, and clanging cymbals materialized out of thin air; heavenly music spontaneously played — all supposedly produced by a loved one seeking to communicate from the other side. On occasion, erotic encounters took place between the sitter and a spirit, often leading to sexual arousal and orgasm.

Harry Houdini, arguably the world's best-known magician, spent twenty years investigating physical mediums and exposing them as quacks. He often demanded that séances be held in the light of day, and as a result, all physical manifestations ceased. At other times, he simply exposed the "magic tricks" the spiritualist used to produce physical effects.[5]

Houdini rarely failed to discredit a medium. For example, Anna Eva Fay (1851–1927) was the most famous physical medium of the era. To show that she did not use trickery to move objects, she sat on a chair inside a custom-built wooden box with her hands and feet protruding through holes and bound by rope. As she slipped into feigned unconsciousness, spirits made their presence known by ringing bells — seemingly unaided by human effort. Sir William Crookes, a renowned British scientist, tested her and proclaimed that Eva Fay was an authentic medium. Some years later, however, Washington Irving Bishop, Fay's assistant and confidant of many years, broke his silence and explained how she accomplished all her feats. She eventually confessed to Houdini, who was about to expose her publicly.

On another occasion, Houdini confronted Mina Crandon (1888–1941), known to her clientele as "Margery the Medium." A vivacious Boston socialite from exclusive Beacon Hill, she claimed to be the conduit through which her deceased brother Walter could speak.

---

4. Ectoplasm is supposedly the so-called spiritual essence of life.

5. In *Miracle Mongers and Their Methods* (New York: Dutton, 1920) and *A Magician among the Spirits* (New York: Harper, 1924), Harry Houdini recounts his campaign early in the twentieth century to expose phony spiritualists.

Operating in the darkness of her séance parlor, all manner of physical manifestations occurred and messages were received. Mina was the talk of New England. Tested several times by eminent scientists, she fooled them all. But she did not succeed in fooling Houdini, who spotted and exposed her trickery.

Houdini was not the only one to expose fraudulent Spiritualists. Madame Helena Blavatsky (1831–1891), founder of the Theosophical Society, was caught cheating during a séance in India. As a result, she was forced to flee the country. Some years later her housekeeper came forward and revealed Blavatsky's modus operandi. The prestigious Society of Psychical Research in Britain henceforth conducted an extensive investigation and concluded the mystic was an unabashed charlatan.

Some of Europe's greatest scientists hailed Eusapia Palladino (1854–1918) to be a great medium of renown.[6] Had they known that early in her life Palladino was married to a traveling magician who taught her all the physical and psychological ploys of the trade, they may have changed their opinion. She produced spirit slate writing, carried hidden objects under her clothing, used her foot to tip the séance table, and her toes to ring bells. While she may have fooled most scientists, she could not dupe professional magicians. When they placed her in secure restraints, she was unable to produce any physical manifestations.

Leonora Piper (1857–1950) was exposed when her two spirit guides, Dr. Pehnuit (a deceased French physician) and George Pellew (a native of Greece), could not answer questions addressed to them in their respective native tongues. Her career soon ended. In 1901, during an interview with the *New York Herald*, Mrs. Piper acknowledged that the source of her mediumistic talents was terrestrial and not celestial.

---

6. Psychologist Joseph Jastrow was the exception. In his book *The Psychology of Conviction: A Study of Beliefs and Attitudes* (New York: Houghton Mifflin, 1918), 101–27, Jastrow included an entire chapter that exposed Eusapia Palladino's tricks.

To avoid further scrutiny and detection, fraudulent spiritualists decided to control their surroundings. They formed self-contained spiritualist camps or communities patterned after revivalist camp-grounds but with restricted admittance. These encampments served as safe havens, where seekers could receive guidance from the great beyond and learn to develop their own psychic powers. Three of the most popular are Lily Dale, Cassadaga, and Camp Chesterfield.

Spiritualist Camps

Lily Dale, about sixty miles south of Buffalo, is the oldest spiritualist camp in America. Founded in 1879 to promote Spiritualism as a religion, the private community has five hundred permanent residents, plus a post office, hotel, cafeteria, library, museum, volunteer fire department, and two churches. The Fox sisters' cottage now sits on the property and draws over 200,000 visitors yearly from around the world.[7]

Lectures and healing services are held daily. Spiritual counseling and trance sittings are offered on an appointment basis.[8] The head-quarters of the National Spiritualist Association of Churches (founded 1893) is located on the site and offers ordination to Spiritualist pastors and ecclesiastical certification to Spiritualist churches.

Cassadaga, located on fifty-seven acres of land on the outskirts of Orlando, Florida, was founded in 1894 by George Colby (1848–1933) and inspired by his visit to Lily Dale. Like its counterpart in New York, Cassadaga is an incorporated township with all the amenities and spiritualistic services one could desire. Because of its warm climate and proximity to Disney World, it has become a popular year-round tourist attraction.

---

7. For a comprehensive history of Lily Dale, see Christine Wicker, *Lily Dale: The True Story of the Town That Talks to the Dead* (New York: HarperCollins, 2003).

8. Some of the past guest lecturers have included such well-known psychics as Arthur Ford, Deepak Chopra, and Kevin Ryerson.

Camp Chesterfield was founded in 1886 by traveling mesmerist and phrenologist John Westerfield. After the death of his fourteen-year-old son, he visited several spiritualist camps in an effort to contact the boy's spirit. Seeking to provide a similar service for the folks of Indiana, he started the campground featuring a unique Cathedral of the Woods. A full-service community, the campground is home to Chesterfield Seminary and the Indiana Association of Spiritualists, which offers certification in healing and ordination for Spiritualist ministers.

Most Spiritualist camps are havens of corruption and scandalous deception. Occasionally, an investigative reporter will sneak into a spiritualist camp, observe the shenanigans, and write an exposé based on firsthand observations. Although these journalists publish their findings, little legal action is ever taken because most Spiritualist camps function as religious denominations.

I wanted to visit a Spiritualist camp for myself to determine whether the reports were accurate. But I would have to wait another few years before the opportunity arrived.[9]

The Unusual Case of Lamar Keene

The Psychic Mafia is the autobiography of Lamar Keene as told to Allen Spraggett, the Canadian television personality and journalist who hosted the Bishop Pike séance with Arthur Ford (see chap. 4).[10] Keene recounts his rise to fame as a pastor of a large Spiritualist church. At the start of his career, the young and naïve trance medium sought guidance from the spirits but soon learned his colleagues relied on unscrupulous means to gather information on their clients. He fol-

9. I eventually took a group of students to Cassadaga in the summer of 2000. We toured the grounds and encountered one resident who attempted to pass off a mentalism trick as genuine psychic ability, but we had no paranormal experiences.

10. M. Lamar Keene, *The Psychic Mafia* (New York: St. Martin's, 1976).

lowed suit. As his reputation grew among physical mediums, Keene was invited to work at Camp Chesterfield and eventually joined its board of directors.

At the height of his popularity, Keene started having pangs of conscience. As his private life deteriorated, the guilt-ridden medium considered suicide. A mutual friend introduced him to William V. Rauscher, a Lutheran pastor, a prominent member of the Spiritual Frontiers Fellowship, and a friend to Arthur Ford. Rauscher, an expert mentalist and a member of the Society of American Magicians (SAM),[11] quickly discerned that Keene used deception in the darkened séance room. Keene was suspicious of Rauscher, but when he learned they both were Masonic brothers, a friendship developed. Over time, Keene unloaded his burden and confessed that he had spent the last thirteen years as a fraudulent medium. Rauscher convinced Keene to share his story and introduced him to Allen Spraggett, a gifted writer who transformed his story into a full-length biography. Rauscher wrote the foreword.

One of Keene's more interesting revelations was that the camp psychics kept files on every client. Pertinent information such as names of relatives, family physicians, place of birth, spouse's occupation, family or health problems, worries and concerns, etc., was collected and placed in a file that was regularly updated and shared with other subscribing mediums around the country. This collection of data was known as the Blue Book. As a result, whenever clients visited other psychics in the network, they received consistent readings. As new information was learned about a client, it was added to the Blue Book. This was nothing more than an antiquated version of the hot reading.

Keene also revealed that Camp Chesterfield psychics hid the truth of their dishonest practices even from their spouses, children, and closest friends, all of whom thought them to be genuine spiritualists with paranormal gifts.

---

11. SAM is one of two major organizations for magicians. The other is the International Brotherhood of Magicians (IBM).

Soon after *The Psychic Mafia* was released in 1976, Keene received death threats, and in 1979, he was the target of an assassination attempt. Keene was shot several times, and his femoral artery was severed. After a prolonged hospital stay, Keene changed his name, moved to another city, and operated a small business until his death at age fifty-nine in 1998.

The story seemed like a work of fiction, but I knew Spraggett and Rauscher to be careful and trustworthy researchers who checked their facts before going to publication. They were not antipsychic crusaders but true believers. Although they knew Keene's story might give spiritualism a black eye, it had to be told. Readers, they said, needed to be warned against fraud and taught to discern between real psychics and pseudopsychics.

After reading *The Psychic Mafia*, I wondered if Spraggett or Rauscher had written other books. To my surprise, I found that they had coauthored *Arthur Ford: The Man Who Talked with the Dead*, a biography of Arthur Ford, a decade earlier.[12] Why had I not heard of this book before?[13] I needed to get a copy. Maybe I could unearth something new about Ford and possibly his relationship with Ted Swager, his protégé and my friend!

---

12. Allen Spraggett with William V. Rauscher, *Arthur Ford: The Man Who Talked with the Dead* (New York: New American Library, 1973).

13. When I looked over Olga's reading list, it was left off. I was soon to learn why.

13

THE MAN WHO SPOKE
TO THE DEAD

Hailed as the greatest medium of the twentieth century, Arthur Ford was in a class by himself. I thought I had read every book and article written by or about him; so, you can only imagine my surprise and excitement to discover *The Man Who Talked with the Dead*. It was a real eye-opener!

When Arthur Ford died in 1971, he left his entire library, personal files, and volumes of correspondence to Rev. William V. Rauscher, his friend and literary genius. Rauscher planned to use the materials and his own recollections to write Ford's authorized biography.

Rauscher invited Allen Spraggett to join the project, and they waded through each piece of paper at their disposal. This included multiple boxes containing Ford's letters and diaries. It was a treasure trove of information. One box stood out among the others. It held several manila folders that were oddly labeled "poems." Turning to Spraggett, the bemused Rauscher said, "I never knew Arthur liked poetry."

What they found inside, however, were not poems at all but scores of neatly clipped newspaper articles and handwritten research notes that Ford had collected on his clients! Several concerned Bishop Pike and *predated* the spellbinding televised séance. In fact, the exact same material that Ford relayed to Bishop Pike from "the other side" actually had an earthly origin.

Rauscher's jaw dropped as he let out a gasp. Here was incontrovertible evidence that Ford had cheated. There was no way around it.

To Rauscher's shock and dismay, Arthur Ford — his hero whom he entertained in his home and sat beside at Spiritual Frontiers Fellowship (SFF) board meetings, and whose funeral he preached — was as much a fraud as Lamar Keene!

When Rauscher and Spraggett questioned Ford's personal secretary about the discovery, he initially acted surprised, but faced with the evidence, he acknowledged that he helped Ford collect data on all his clients. Ford cryptically called these notes and clippings his "poems." As his health deteriorated and he sensed death was imminent, he ordered his "poems" destroyed. The assistant did as instructed but somehow overlooked a single box — the one that contained files on Bishop Pike.

Ford's lifelong claim that while in trance his knowledge came from Fletcher, his spirit guide, was no truer than the Fox sisters' claim that Charles Rosna was their source!

Rauscher and Spraggett debated whether or not to include this newfound information in the upcoming biography. How might the revelation negatively impact the reputation of the SFF or, worse yet, destroy many people's belief in survival after death?

In the end, they decided to tell the whole story! To soften the blow for readers, Rauscher hypothesized that Ford was a *true* medium but didn't want to disappoint his sitters. So, he conducted research on them and their deceased loved ones before every séance just in case he was unable to slip into a trance on the day of the sitting. To me Rauscher's explanation was a stretch.[1]

---

1. With the passing of time, Rauscher came to believe that Ford's cheating started early in his career and continued until his death, casting doubt on

This revelation sickened me. If his mentor cheated, the protégé Ted Swager likely did the same. I concluded that the odds of Ted being a genuine spiritualist medium were slim indeed. This was disconcerting. When we first met on the campus of Wesley Seminary decades before, I was convinced Ted had a sixth sense that enabled him to transcend the veil of death. He was my hero, and I wanted to be like him. When I heard Dennis Bennett preach on the demonic nature of the occult, my perspective changed. Concerned for Ted's eternal soul, I reached out and urged him to abandon spiritualism. I was thrilled when he did, only to be heartbroken when he reverted back to mediumship. But now I felt a different emotion — anger, red-hot, blazing anger!

If Ted was indeed a deceiver — no different from Arthur Ford, the Fox sisters, or the dozens of mediums Houdini exposed — that was a different matter altogether. I felt betrayed.

I wanted to lash out and confront Ted. I wanted to look him in the eyes and ask him directly if he knew about Ford's secret files and if he, too, had a similar set of files on his clients. Unfortunately, since it was prior to the Internet, I had no way of knowing Ted's current whereabouts or how to contact him.

Then, in 1991, I received a letter from my mother along with an enclosed article from the *Baltimore Sun*: "Retired Minister Explores Realm of Visions."[2] My heart skipped a beat as I read that Ted, now sixty-one years old and retired, was again living in Maryland. The article revealed that Ted and Lois had started a new nonprofit called the Spiritual Research and Development Institute "to help people understand and deal with psychic phenomena." It also mentioned that

whether Ford ever possessed psychic ability. See William V. Rauscher, *Religion, Magic, and the Supernatural* (Woodbury, NJ: Mystic Light, 2006), 116, 524, 535. Rauscher later wrote *The Houdini Code Mystery: A Spirit Secret Solved* (Pasadena, CA: Magic Words, 2000), devoted entirely to examining Ford's claim in 1928 that he made contact with Houdini from beyond the grave.

2. Angela Gambill, "Retired Minister Explores Realm of Visions," *Baltimore Sun*, April 23, 1991.

Ted was giving six weekly lectures at the Crofton Public Library, free and open to the public. In the first session, he touted his relationship with Arthur Ford, told of his past successes as a trance medium, and explained the significance of interpreting dreams and visions. He also suggested that most people hunger for spiritual reality because churches do not meet their needs.

To his credit, he warned of the dangers of becoming obsessed with the paranormal. Lois added, "It's subtle. More and more is taken from you without you realizing it. Our family was almost destroyed." I remembered clearly all the hardships the Swagers endured as Ted pursued his dream of succeeding Arthur Ford and becoming America's top trance medium.

Ted clearly warned his library audience against aggressively attempting to contact the dead. He said the Bible condemned such efforts, but then, in a seemingly contradictory statement, he admitted to recently "having visions of the dead." In the end, Ted concluded that paranormal experiences (in and of themselves) "are neutral and we should not seek after them, but if they happen, we should try to understand their meaning."

The article disclosed that Ted was now living in Shady Side, Maryland. I sat down immediately and wrote a letter, bringing him up to date on my ministry and inquiring about his life and family. I then asked in a matter-of-fact way if he knew about Arthur Ford's cheating. I assumed Ted must have read *The Man Who Talked with the Dead* since he was Ford's heir apparent, but I was flummoxed why he never mentioned it to me. Finally, I got to the real crux of my letter and asked him directly if he too dug up information on sitters before giving them a trance reading.

It was simply inconceivable to me that Ted was in the dark about Ford's unscrupulous activities. I wanted to know if Ford taught him mentalism tricks or the necessity of hot reading in order to fool his clients. I closed my letter with a plea for Ted to come clean and admit that spiritualism was a scam (just like the Fox sisters and Lamar Keene did). I added, "As the protégé of the most renowned medium of all time, your admission will carry weight and keep other innocents from being duped by spiritualist con artists." I offered, "If you will confess your deception, I will write a book and tell your side of the story."

I don't know how I expected Ted to respond, but I hoped he would confirm my conclusions that most mediums were tricksters.

I did not hear back from Ted until November 19, 1994 — nearly three years later! His letter opened with a brief update on his family, his retirement, and some lectures he was giving at a local community college. He launched into an accusation of his own and charged me with being "obsessed with too much negativism aimed at debunking and not emphasizing the positive side" of psychic phenomena. He added, "I . . . find your use of a negative ('your mentalism act') inappropriate. You seem to be saying that ESP and psychic phenomena do not exist and, of course, I disagree with your assumption." He responded to my invitation for him to "come clean" by saying, "Regarding my sending you my testimony for use in your book, I do not feel led to burn my incense on your altar."

Despite our differences, Ted thanked me for writing and said he hoped his reply would not damage our friendship. He welcomed further correspondence.

My arrogant and accusatory tone had obviously offended my friend. I decided to write back and take a slightly different approach.

In early 1995, I sent Ted a follow-up letter. I explained the path my own spiritual journey had taken up to that point, especially my shock to discover the truth about Arthur Ford. Then I asked Ted what he thought when he first heard of Ford's files. I wanted to get Ted "on the record" even if he wasn't ready to confess to fraud himself. I again asked if he would like me to write his story.

The weeks turned into months, and I did not hear from Ted. I interpreted his silence as an admission of guilt and concluded that he was as much a spiritualist fraud as his mentor!

With no word from Ted, I turned to others who knew both Ford and Swager, hoping they could offer me additional information. I was on a mission to blow the lid off spiritualism!

After a prolonged search, I obtained the personal address of Irene Hughes, the famous Chicago seer, who first encouraged Ted to develop his psychic powers. In the spring of 1996, I wrote to her, explained my research, and asked if she remembered the meeting at Professor Ed Bauman's house three decades earlier. I wanted to make sure Ted's account was accurate and invited her to comment on Arthur Ford's cheating. I received a three-page typed response from Ms. Hughes on July 22, 1996, acknowledging that she knew Ted and had indeed advised him to explore ESP and expand his psychic horizons. But she also confided that she always doubted Ted's sincerity. According to her recollection, he was not happy as a small-town pastor and wanted to achieve fame and fortune as a medium. She was not surprised by the news that Ted renounced spiritualism and later returned to it, adding that he was "confused about many things."

Throughout the letter, Irene Hughes criticized many of her contemporaries while exalting herself as America's foremost seer. I was put off by her self-promotion and found little else helpful. I came to realize that psychics on the whole are a competitive bunch and jealous of each other.

Next, I wrote to William Rauscher, hoping he, more than others, could answer my inquiries. But instead, his response was ambiguous at best. He knew from various sources that Ford had mentored Ted, but Rauscher had never met Ted personally. Regarding Ford's research files and spurious séances, he described Ford as "very complex" and "many faceted," adding that he was "not a happy man, but a tormented soul." Rauscher believed Ford likely possessed legitimate psychic powers but was "a scoundrel" and not above cheating. If this was Rauscher's evaluation of Arthur Ford, the dean of American spiritualists, then what should I conclude about Ted?

I needed to find someone who knew Ted in the early days of his ascendancy. In my research I kept coming across the name Frank Tribbe, a North Carolinian who served on the SFF national board for twenty-seven years, linking him to the organization's founding. For the past two decades he served as editor of the SFF journal. A close friend of Arthur Ford, he spent a month with him each year at Ford's home in Miami until Ford's death. They were the closest of confidants and talked weekly by phone.

I wrote Tribbe a long letter explaining my interests and concerns. He replied quickly and said he knew Ted when Ted served as chairman of the SFF chapter in Washington, DC. Regarding Swager's legitimacy, Tribbe mentioned that his wife, Audre, had a "very evidential" reading with Ted, who disclosed things about her past that could not have been researched. Tribbe was convinced Ted was the real McCoy. However, he said, "I never saw them (Ford and Swager) together or heard Ted mentioned outside D.C."[3]

I contacted many others in an attempt to determine whether Swager was dishonest like his mentor and whether he was merely a mentalist posing as a psychic and spiritualist. The responses were less than satisfying for many reasons, but mainly because nearly three decades had passed since Ford and Swager were together. Memories had faded over time.

Then, out of the blue, I opened my mailbox and found a letter from Ted. It was dated August 6, 1996. It had been over eighteen months since our last correspondence. He asked me to forgive him for waiting so long to write but said he and his family had been inundated with medical concerns. Ted went on to discuss a terrible accident and a serious disease, along with prolonged hospitalizations of two sons, adding that he had suffered two recent heart attacks. Then he added: "The other reason my reply has been delayed is not that I am unwilling but I would like to know more about what you are going to say in your book and how the material you think I can offer would actually be used." Ted also voiced concern regarding the editing process and mentioned that he had been misquoted in the past and had his words twisted to support the author's views and not his own. In closing he wrote, "I, too,

---

3. Contrary to Tribbe's recollection, I have been able to document through SFF newsletters from 1969 to 1972 that Ted had traveled widely up and down the East Coast and into Middle America giving lectures and readings.

feel there is still much to be said about this area of interest and my message is as much directed to the church as to the gullibility of the general populace. I hope you will answer or call."

I felt terrible. Had I misjudged Ted's delay in responding to my follow-up letter as an admission of guilt, when in reality he was just going through a prolonged string of serious health and family problems? Did his "dark night of the soul" hinder him from answering in a timely fashion?

The tone between Ted's first and second letter was like night and day. He originally said he was unwilling to cooperate with my efforts. Now, he seemed more open.

It took me a day or two to evaluate his letter more objectively. Finally, I realized that Ted's response, while it once again moved me emotionally, did not answer my questions. Ted did not address my query about Ford's files or if he even knew about them. Additionally, he avoided my question about his own cheating. Why did he not speak about these issues? Was he simply reluctant to put his thoughts on paper, lest I use them against him? For whatever reason, he sidestepped the real issues.

Quite frankly, after spending decades of research into the nature of the paranormal, I was exhausted and no closer to finding answers than when I had first begun. It was like trying to nail Jell-O to the wall.

Are paranormal gifts and manifestations God-given as the SFF claim? Or satanic counterfeits as charismatics and evangelicals believe? Or mentalism tricks used to dupe and scam the gullible as professional magicians allege? I concluded that maybe there were no definitive answers.

I glanced again at Ted's letter and read his closing words: "I hope you will answer or call."

Instead, I laid it aside.

✦

In the late 1990s, my wife and I became empty nesters with three sons off to college or in graduate school. After serving as minister of the same church for ten years, I was on the verge of burnout and considered a career change. While attending a large convention, I ran into a few old colleagues from Criswell College who encouraged me to return to the classroom. A new administration was in place, and the college was no longer embroiled in denominational politics. I decided to test the waters and agreed to teach a few evening classes as an adjunct while continuing my pastorate. I soon rediscovered my love for the classroom and daily interaction with students.

In 1998, I accepted a full-time faculty position, which turned into an additional twenty-five-year tenure. Students in large numbers enrolled in my courses, especially the ones dealing with the occult, cults, and apologetics.

As we faced a new century, not even a psychic could have anticipated the future. First, we faced the Y2K crisis — an anticipated crash of all computers worldwide, which some wild-eyed Bible thumpers announced would usher in the Apocalypse. When we woke on New Year's Day and discovered that everything was intact and secure, we uttered a collective sigh of relief. But it was short-lived. On September 11, 2001, two planes commandeered by terrorists crashed into the Twin Towers at the World Trade Center. The world as we knew it had changed overnight. Americans were angry and stressed, and much of my time in the classroom was spent counseling distraught students.

As for Ted Swager, he was always on my mind. But I still had not responded to his evasive letter.

PART 4

14

MIND OVER MATTER

In 2002, I began to teach an early Sunday morning Bible class at a large church in Dallas. To ensure we got up on time, Lynn and I set our clock radio for 6 a.m. and programmed it to NPR. Each week we woke to a soothing voice and soft background music: "This is David Freudberg and you are listening to *Humankind*." On each thirty-minute broadcast the host interviewed guests from all walks of life on an array of topics such as peace, health care, social conscience, mind-body medicine, justice, and meditation. *Humankind* became part of our Sunday ritual and set the tone for our day.

The first program told the remarkable case of Henry Green, a heart patient with little hope of survival. Admitted to a university hospital, he lay weak and incapacitated, biding his time on earth. In the course of their rounds, a staff physician and his team of interns stopped by Mr. Green's room. After examining the patient's chart, the doctor looked knowingly at his interns and commented in a matter-of-fact tone, "Mr. Green has a galloping heart." They each nodded and within seconds left the room. Mr. Green immediately perked up and thought to himself, *If my heart is galloping, it must be getting stronger.* His spirit soared, and he felt better instantly.

As his feeble body responded positively to the doctor's suggestion, his labored breathing eased and he began to move his arms and legs without difficulty. Feeling stronger and healthier than he had in months, the bedridden patient got up, dressed, checked himself out of the hospital, and never returned.

What made Mr. Green's case so unique was that he misinterpreted the meaning of the doctor's comment. In medical parlance, a "galloping heart" usually refers to an abnormal heart rhythm, and in this case, pointed to a serious case of heart failure. But Mr. Green didn't understand it that way. He took the comments to mean just the opposite — his heart was getting stronger![1]

Here was a fascinating case of mind over matter!

Lynn and I became regular listeners to *Humankind*. Each program expanded our knowledge of the mind's vast power to accomplish the impossible. One episode, an interview with Herbert Benson, MD, caused me to explore the paranormal from a new perspective. Benson, a respected cardiologist and associate professor at Harvard University Medical School, was a pioneer in mind-body medicine. For several years he conducted scientific research into the medical benefits of meditation. To his surprise, he discovered that twenty minutes of daily meditation lowered blood pressure and led to significant physical and psychological benefits. It did not matter if practitioners were religious or atheist, young or old, educated or uneducated; the results were the same. Benson asked his Harvard colleagues and scientists from other schools to check his testing procedures, data, and conclusions. He then conducted additional double-blind tests to make sure the results could be replicated. Benson's findings broke new ground in the field of mind-body research, and he published his findings in peer-reviewed journals. To reach a wider audience, he wrote *The Relaxation Response*, where he told his story and explained his findings in simple terms.[2] It became an instant best seller.

1. Cardiologist Bernard Lown, MD, recounts the story of his patient's amazing recovery on *Humankind*, episode #23. I have used a pseudonym rather than the patient's real name. The broadcast is available at https://www.humanmedia .org/product/lost-art-healing/.

2. Herbert Benson with Miriam Z. Klipper, *The Relaxation Response* (New York: Morrow, 1975).

In the book Benson explains that daily meditation elicits what he calls the "relaxation response," a condition that is opposite of the *fight-or-flight* response triggered in the brain. When faced with a threatening situation, our body normally produces an increased amount of adrenaline that helps us resist or flee danger; but afterward we are left physically drained. When activated, the relaxation response enables us to think rationally and act calmly when confronted by peril.[3]

Once his findings were scientifically validated, Benson prescribed a daily dose of *meditation* along with *medication* for all his heart patients. He instructed them to find a quiet place, clear their minds, and begin to breathe slowly from the diaphragm. On the inhale they were to say a word silently (such as "peace"), and on the exhale do the same. This repetition placed the practitioner in a serene state (i.e., an altered state of consciousness) and elicited the relaxation response. In his book Benson also addressed many misconceptions people have about meditation, such as (1) meditation is an Eastern religious practice that promotes pantheism; (2) it opens the door to demon possession; and (3) as a therapy, it falls into the category of pseudoscience.

When I discovered that Herbert Benson (1935–2022) had written several other books on the power of the mind, I ordered them all.[4]

Benson also conducted research into the placebo effect, which refers to the positive outcome of an intervention, drug, or procedure,

---

3. The Gospels reveal that on many occasions Jesus faced danger yet remained composed. For example, while his disciples freaked out when caught in a violent storm, Jesus slept like a baby (Matt. 8:23–27). When encountering mortal threats, Jesus did not pull a sword to defend himself (fight), or run for his life (flight), but remained cool (Luke 4:16–30; John 10:38–39). Nor did he call for angels to rescue him or beg for his life when standing before Pontius Pilate (Matt. 26:53). He seemed to have everything under control.

4. Including, Herbert Benson with William Proctor, *Beyond the Relaxation Response* (New York: Times Books, 1984); Herbert Benson with Marg Stark, *Timeless Healing: The Power and Biology of Belief* (New York: Scribner's Sons, 1990); Herbert Benson with William Proctor, *The Breakout Principle* (New York: Scribner's Sons, 2003).

regardless of its efficacy, based solely on the patient's expectations.[5] If a person believes a treatment will work, it usually does. When a patient has faith (even in a quack doctor or an inert sugar pill), the immune system often kicks in, chemicals are released, and the body responds accordingly.[6] Expectations become reality.

What triggers the placebo effect? The answers vary. Sometimes it is a convincing and well-produced pharmaceutical commercial that is aired repeatedly during one's favorite TV show or the color of a prescribed medication (purple pills work best). At other times it is a doctor's reputation, words of encouragement, or bedside manner.

When Mr. Green misinterpreted his doctor's words about a "galloping heart," his faith kicked in! He rose up and walked.

Both the "relaxation response" and the "placebo effect" attest to the intricate relationship of mind and body. The former is the result of *right breathing*. The latter is the result of *positive expectation*.

For me to accept Benson's hypothesis and conclusions meant I had to adjust my thinking. As a former "cult buster," I warned of the dangers of meditation and misguided faith, but after hearing the Benson interview (and subsequently reading his books), I realized I needed to do more research. Maybe Benson was right and I was wrong!

If quiet breathing can lower blood pressure and a doctor's misconstrued words can reverse a life-threatening heart ailment, what else can the mind accomplish?

As a baseball player, I knew the mental aspect of the game was just as important, if not more so, than the physical one.[7] This explains why some players with superior athletic ability fail to perform under pressure and others with average skills rise to the occasion. Confidence

---

5. We see examples of this every day. A child skins her knee and comes crying to Mommy, who kisses it and makes it better. The power of the placebo effect is based on trust and expectation.

6. The placebo effect is evidence of the biological power of belief.

7. Yogi Berra, the New York Yankees' Hall of Fame catcher, allegedly once said, "Baseball is 90 percent mental. The other half is physical." While mathematically incorrect, this Yogism drives home the point that the mental game of baseball is essential to top performance.

(faith) and relaxation at the plate (proper breathing) give some players a competitive edge.

I had not considered, however, the possibility that our minds might also affect other areas of life.[8] If the combination of relaxation and faith can heal the body and enable a ballplayer to outperform his ability, what else might it do? Could some unexplained psychic phenomena be attributed to the power of mind over matter? The possibilities seemed unlimited yet unsettling.

I decided to study the relationship between the human mind and body, an investigation that would extend for twenty years and yield life-changing results.

CENTERING PRAYER

As I delved more deeply into meditation and the power of the mind, I came across the works of Thomas Keating, a Cistercian priest, and his teachings on "centering prayer."[9] Unlike other forms of prayer (e.g., intercession, petition, praise, etc.), centering prayer involves entering a contemplative state and responds to God's invitation to "Be still, and know that I am God!" (Ps. 46:10). The daily ritual enables a person to quiet all thoughts and remove exterior noise and clutter, while experiencing the presence of God.

According to Keating, centering prayer includes relaxing in a comfortable chair and breathing slowly and rhythmically while mentally repeating a sacred word or phrase (e.g., "Jesus," "Abba," "love," "peace," etc.)[10] on the inhale and exhale,[11] letting go of all thoughts on each

---

8. According to the Christian Scriptures, Jesus often attributed healing to a person's faith (Matt. 9:29; Mark 5:29; 10:52). On other occasions, the Bible says he could not heal "because of their unbelief" (Matt. 13:58).

9. Thomas Keating, *Intimacy with God* (New York: Crossroad, 1994), and *Open Mind, Open Heart: The Contemplative Dimension of the Gospel* (New York: Continuum, 2003).

10. Keating, *Open Mind, Open Heart*, 43–51.

11. Richard Rohr, a Franciscan monk and advocate of contemplative prayer, recommends using the sacred name of Yahweh, Israel's god, when breathing in

successive breath; if thoughts return, let them pass like a boat sailing down the river, and then return to the sacred word.[12]

Most people who practice twenty to thirty minutes a day experience a sense of tranquillity, lose track of time, and move from a state of *doing and knowing* to a state of *being*.[13] They feel like they are entirely in "the moment." Most say they sense a oneness with God and are filled with great joy.[14] The centering prayer session slowly comes to an end on its own and leaves the person in a state of calm. This feeling may last from several minutes to an hour.

Centering prayer helps us get in touch with God by altering our consciousness. After prolonged practice, participants eventually begin to sense God's closeness throughout the day. As their faith is emboldened, they stop relying on their own ingenuity and start trusting God to guide them intuitively.

It didn't take a rocket scientist to recognize the affinity between the relaxation response and centering prayer. Both involve deep breathing and the repetition of a chosen word. Both lead to an altered state of consciousness. While Benson views meditation as a way of attaining physical benefits, Keating views it as a way of experiencing God. I doubt that Benson and Keating ever met or even knew of each other. They lived in two different worlds. Benson was a man of science and Keating a man of religion, yet both used the same techniques to attain their respective goals.

My mind went back to my first visit to the Golden Lotus Temple (Washington, DC) and listening to Achariya Peter extol the benefits of yoga, leading to enlightenment and ultimately union with God. What Peter taught sounded similar to Keating's centering prayer, except Peter defined God in Hindu terms. Otherwise, they differed very

---

and out. On the inhale, silently say "Yah," and on the exhale, "weh." This keeps our mind focused on God.

12. Keating, *Open Mind, Open Heart*, 35–36.

13. Keating, *Open Mind, Open Heart*, 37.

14. The divine presence is rarely achieved in the first session but often comes after consecutive days of centering prayer.

little. Both emphasized a rhythmic breathing from the diaphragm and repeating a mantra or sacred word until the practitioner loses conscious awareness of his or her surroundings and experiences oneness with God. The encounter with the divine usually does not happen overnight but comes through dedication to the discipline.[15]

On the surface there is little difference between Eastern and Western forms of mysticism. The practices are basically the same, although the vocabulary differs. Devotees of the various traditions have one thing in common — they all enter an altered state of consciousness (ASC).[16]

My Sabbatical Year

My daily schedule was jam-packed. Besides preparing for my regular college lectures and the weekly adult Bible study, I became editor of the *Criswell Theological Review* (*CTR*), a semiannual scholarly journal devoted to academic research in biblical and theological studies. Soliciting, editing, and proofreading articles; checking galleys; distributing the journal; and maintaining a subscriber list were time consuming and overwhelming. By 2005, I knew I needed a break; so, I petitioned the college for a yearlong sabbatical. It was granted with the provision that I take on a research project.

I had wanted to work on a second doctorate for some time and discovered that universities in the United Kingdom offered postgraduate degrees based solely on original research, culminating in a 100,000-word thesis. I applied and was accepted into the University of Wales,

---

15. Some entrepreneurial master yogis claim to teach their students a shortcut to oneness — usually for a price!

16. Benson taught the same principles, but as a scientist he did not promote seeking an encounter with God. Ironically, Benson's research into meditation began by observing and testing followers of Transcendental Meditation. He later traveled to Tibet to do the same with Buddhist monks. As a scientist, however, he was not concerned with subjective religious experiences one might have during the meditative state. Rather, he wanted to determine whether meditation has physical benefits.

Lampeter. In my naïveté and arrogance, I thought I could complete the program in a short time, but I quickly realized the process normally takes from four to six years![17] I also discovered that the quality of scholarship required of a British PhD far surpassed that required for my doctorate at California Graduate School of Theology.

My sabbatical year was more grueling than my regular schedule as a college professor. I spent several hours a day reading and researching for my thesis. I needed a sabbatical from my sabbatical! To wind down, rather than watch television in the evenings, Lynn and I enrolled in a free online hypnotism course offered by Hypnosis Motivation Institute (HMI). At first, we did it as a lark — just something to do together — but soon recognized we had stumbled onto a wealth of information. HMI (Tarzana, California) was the first college of hypnotherapy in America to be nationally accredited.

HYPNOSIS AND THE SUBCONSCIOUS MIND

The twelve weekly lessons covered the basics and benefits of hypnotherapy. HMI offered the classes free of charge with hopes that some students might be interested enough to enroll in the advanced two-year *tuition-based* course of study leading to a diploma in hypnotherapy.

John Kappas (1925–2002) founded HMI on the controversial proposition that everyone is hypnotizable[18] and can profit from hypnotherapy. In 1973, he defined the term "hypnotherapist" for the *Federal Dictionary of Occupational Titles*, which is still in print and classifies hypnotherapy as an occupation.

Kappas theorized that the human mind operates at two levels. First, the *conscious* or critical mind — that is, logic, reason, and willpower — guides our thoughts and activities during the daylight hours. The con-

---

17. I was fifty-nine years old when I matriculated, and when I passed my orals five years later, I was sixty-four.

18. Most psychologists believe that from 25 to 50 percent of all adults are not susceptible to a hypnotic trance.

scious mind thinks analytically and motivates us to act in a rational manner. Most of us believe we are levelheaded and can solve our problems through common sense and willpower. This is not the case.

Second, the *subconscious* mind determines approximately 80 percent of our behaviors and actions. It is the storehouse of our experiences and ingrained habits that have accumulated over a lifetime and form us into the people we are today. When we attempt to overcome long-standing problems and embedded hang-ups such as addictions, fears, phobias, anger, lack of self-worth, etc., through sheer willpower alone, we usually fail. For example, few of us have the ability to quit smoking. We automatically lift a cigarette to our lips without thinking twice. Habits are second nature because they are entrenched in our subconscious minds. To solve these kinds of difficult issues, we must deal with them at the subconscious level. This is where hypnosis can help.

Hypnosis is a means of accessing the subconscious mind.

Through the process of rhythmic breathing, concentration on a fixed object, and following the hypnotherapist's verbal suggestions, a person slowly slips into an altered state. As the conscious mind shuts down, the hypnotherapist accesses the subconscious mind, probes the sources of one's problems, and offers suggestions that trigger the imagination, leading to a solution.[19] These verbal prompts come in the form of posthypnotic suggestions that are carried out during the wakened state.

A person can also learn *self-hypnosis*. Using the same techniques — deep breathing, relaxation, and concentrating on a focal point or word — one can slip into an altered state. A powerful suggestion, either predetermined or recorded, can be deposited into the subconscious mind as an aid to behavior modification.[20]

---

19. For example, a person may lack self-worth because in childhood the person's father said, "You'll never make anything of yourself. You'll always be a failure and a disappointment." No matter how hard one tries consciously to overcome, the criticism remains. The subconscious mind must be reprogrammed.

20. Autosuggestions only work at a subconscious level. You can repeat "I am

Lynn and I enjoyed the free HMI course and gained much insight into the human psyche. We wished we could take the advanced track, but the cost of the two-year diploma program was prohibitive at the time. Plus, my sabbatical year was coming to an end in August 2006. Over the summer, I wrote my PhD prospectus and scheduled a meeting with Dr. William Campbell, my University of Wales supervisor who was coming to Philadelphia in November to present a scholarly paper at a conference. He flew in from Wales, and I from Dallas. We enjoyed a working breakfast. After looking over my prospectus, he recommended that I narrow my topic significantly. He also suggested several books to read and said I needed to keep him up to date on my progress. Dr. Campbell was a kindly gentleman and enjoyed mentoring American students. But it was obvious to me (and possibly to him!) that I had bitten off more than I could chew. At sixty years of age, I began to doubt if I had the ability to complete a second doctorate. The road ahead looked long and grueling.

---

not a smoker" all day long with your critical mind with no results. It must take hold first in the subconscious mind.

15

PRACTICE WHAT YOU PREACH!

With my sabbatical ended, it was back to the grindstone. I had just added PhD research to the mix and was busier than ever. Still, I looked forward to the new semester. I was scheduled to teach a course titled "Reaching the Subconscious Mind" and planned to incorporate my latest findings on meditation, yoga, mysticism, hypnosis, centering prayer, and relaxation response into my lecture notes.

More than thirty students enrolled, and the class was an instant hit. I required each student to enroll in the free HMI course, meditate twenty minutes per day following Benson's model as outlined in *The Relaxation Response*, and keep a journal of thoughts, experiences, and questions. We had some lively classroom discussions.

When word spread around campus, many raised their eyebrows and wondered if such a course should be taught at a Christian college. Fortunately, the school president had great faith in me and gave me total freedom in the classroom.

In a bold move, I contacted HMI and told them about my class and how all students were required to watch the HMI streaming videos, and brazenly asked if they would be willing to enroll me in their two-year advanced diploma course at no cost. To my utter surprise, they said yes. For the next two years (2007–2009) Lynn and I spent our evenings glued to the computer. Overall, the quality of the lectures and the materials covered was excellent. I gained as much insight, if not more, into psychology and the mind than I did at the University of Baltimore as a psychology major.

We also began to read books by Milton Erickson, MD (1901–1980), an acclaimed psychiatrist and innovative hypnotherapist. Known as the father of modern hypnosis, Erickson's science-based methods and use of metaphors to reach the subconscious mind changed the face of hypnotherapy. Psychiatry departments in most leading universities have since adopted his approach and consider it the gold standard for training in hypnotherapy. I subsequently enrolled in a workshop taught by Betty Alice Erickson (Erickson's daughter) to learn his unique and nuanced techniques.[1]

Despite the heavy load, I tenaciously continued working on my PhD, and Dr. Campbell patiently guided me along. As I completed each chapter, he read it critically and made recommendations, which I followed to the letter until he was satisfied with the finished product. I finally completed my 340-page thesis and submitted it to the post-graduate office of the University of Wales in the late spring of 2010 and waited with bated breath for a response. A month later I received word that my viva voce (oral exam) would be conducted in the fall before two British scholars who would grill me on its content.

I got in touch with other Wales PhD students who had faced a similar examination. Two were required to make major revisions and undergo a second oral, which added another year to their program and additional tuition costs. The prospect of facing my inquisitors was nerve-racking. So, I made a major decision. *I needed to practice what I preached.*

I immediately began following the daily *relaxation response* protocol for myself. At first, sitting quietly, breathing in and out, and mentally repeating a meaningful word seemed awkward. But before long I

---

1. Subsequently, I was accepted into membership of the American Psychological Association and joined Division 30, Society of Psychological Hypnosis, which promotes hypnosis as a psychological tool.

settled into a routine. The rhythmic breathing calmed my nerves, and the repetition cleared my mind of all thoughts. Within a few minutes I found myself in a serene place where time seemed to stop and all anxiety disappeared. When I returned to consciousness, the peaceful effects lingered. I usually practiced the relaxation response in my office before heading to class. When I did, I entered the classroom stress-free and comfortably interacted with the students. On days when I did not meditate, there was a noticeable difference.

As the date for my oral exam approached, I learned the identity of my examiners and checked them out on the Internet. My internal reader was the newly appointed dean at the University of Wales, and my outside reader was the provost at another university in the United Kingdom. When I discovered that both were members of the Society of Biblical Literature and planned to attend the annual November meeting in Atlanta, I asked Dr. Campbell if it were possible to conduct the oral at the conference site. He made the arrangements.

Lynn and I arrived on the designated date and settled into our hotel room. I immediately began to read over my thesis in anticipation of the questions that my examiners might ask. As the hour approached, Lynn became anxious for me. Two of my sons, each a professor of theology, and also at the conference, wondered how I would fare. As for me, thirty minutes before my appointment, I sat back in my hotel chair and began breathing deeply. Before long I slipped into an altered state. Stillness surrounded me, and my mind was like a calm river. I don't know how to describe it, except to say it was like being in a state of suspended animation, floating effortlessly on a cloud of air — totally relaxed. When I came back to consciousness, I was calm and rested.

I headed downstairs to the conference room and met my examiners. They were fidgety, yet I was at ease and quickly established a rapport with them. The door was closed, and the oral exam began.

One hour passed and then two. Dr. Campbell paced back and forth in the hotel lobby. Lynn sat outside the examination room and waited. My sons had checked on my progress at least twice between conference sessions. What was taking so long?

For nearly three hours my examiners explored my thesis and grilled me on many minute details. I was prepared, and the answers to their questions flowed effortlessly. At the conclusion of the viva voce, the inquisitors approved my thesis and recommended I be granted the PhD from the University of Wales. I was sixty-four years old! When I came out of the conference room to give Lynn and Dr. Campbell the report, they were on pins and needles. But upon hearing the good news, their worried looks melted away and we rejoiced together. Campbell suggested we meet later for a celebration supper. It was a wonderful evening.

The relaxation response really worked! I was living proof.[2] When faced with tough questions often designed to trip me up, I was composed and confident. My mind ran on all cylinders, and my thinking was crystal clear. I surprised myself by some of my responses and wondered, *Where did that came from?* Certainly not from my conscious mind! I had experienced the marvelous power of the subconscious at work.

This led me to ponder, *What if some psychics and trance mediums have the same ability to access resources from the subconscious, which allows them to offer wisdom and insight to their clients and sitters?* If I tapped into the subconscious, why not them? More specifically, What about my friend Ted Swager? Had I judged him too harshly? What if Ted was not a fraud after all, but simply able to retrieve information from his subconscious?[3] What was the difference between Ted entering a trance

---

2. I knew I had to tell others about the relaxation response and the power of the subconscious mind. I decided to devote two issues of the *Criswell Theological Review* (7, no. 2 [Spring 2010]; 8, no. 1 [Fall 2010]) to the mind-body connection, which included articles on the relaxation response, snake handling and the subconscious mind, nature of the soul, hypnosis and the Christian, hypnosis and clergy, interviews with Herbert Benson, among others. Based on this series of journal articles, the National Guild of Hypnotists named me the recipient of the William N. Curtis Award, given to an individual for expanding the understanding of hypnosis and religion.

3. As the reader may recall, after Ted returned to trance work, he informed

and me eliciting the relaxation response? We both reclined, breathed slowly, and limited our focus until our conscious mind receded and the subconscious took over.

For sure, there are many unscrupulous psychics. Some are nothing more than mentalists gone bad who utilize psychological subtleties and misdirection to dupe people. But for me to serve as prosecutor, judge, and jury (i.e., to boldly charge Ted as a fake, pronounce him guilty, and then pass sentence) was unconscionable.

To determine for certain the source of Ted's psychic powers, I needed to do a lot more research.

Dr. Pyke and me that he now believed his paranormal insights and wisdom came from his subconscious mind and not spirits from the other side. At the time, we scoffed at the suggestion and believed he was simply offering an excuse to take up mediumship once again.

16

THE SUBCONSCIOUS MIND
AND BRAINWAVES

In 2012, I was named senior research professor at Criswell College. I stepped down as editor of *CTR* and assumed a lighter teaching load, which gave me ample time to do research and write.[1] I also commenced an in-depth study into the power of the subconscious mind.

MY DISCOVERIES IN BROAD STROKES

Forming valid conclusions about the source and nature of paranormal manifestations is no easy task. Even after decades of research, I still had more questions than answers. My newest research, however, revealed a direct link between the subconscious and the paranormal. In the following pages I share my findings from an additional twelve years

---

1. Over the next decade I wrote *Subversive Meals* (Eugene, OR: Pickwick, 2013); *Heaven on Earth* (Eugene, OR: Harvest House, 2013); *Caesar and the Sacrament* (Eugene, OR: Cascade, 2018); and *Songs of Resistance* (Eugene, OR: Cascade, 2022), and contributed over a dozen chapters to edited works.

of exploring the mind-body connection. These conclusions, I believe, will stand the test of time.

Defining the Subconscious Mind

Popular literature variously defines the subconscious as the soul, the right brain, or the mind that lies just beneath the surface of consciousness. Scientists, theologians, and mystics describe the subconscious from their differing perspectives. For our purposes we will keep things simple.

As humans, we function mentally at two levels: conscious and unconscious.[2] The clearest example is the difference between being awake and being asleep. During the day we are conscious. Our critical mind enables us to think rationally. We don't accept all *so-called* facts at face value or act on everything we learn, hear, or see. They must be tested. For example, if a friend says your hair is on fire, you can check it out and act accordingly. Your friend may be mistaken or might even be playing a joke on you. Your conscious or critical mind sorts out fact from fantasy.

At night we are unconscious of our surroundings. Even during our waking hours, we occasionally slip into a degree of unconsciousness. Something stimulates our imagination and we begin to daydream. While lecturing I often notice a student with a faraway look in her eyes. She sits only a few feet away but doesn't see or hear me. She is unconscious of her surroundings. Instead, she sees herself walking along a beach, hand in hand with her lover. She hears the roar of the waves pounding the shoreline, feels the warm breeze against her face and the sand between her toes. It all seems so real, *but it is not!*

What happened? My student's critical (conscious) mind temporarily took a rest. As her subconscious mind emerged, her five senses

---

2. I use the terms "unconscious" and "subconscious" interchangeably throughout this chapter. Medical professionals prefer the former designation while laypeople typically use the latter.

receded into the background. To jar her back into reality, I must tap on her desk or loudly call out her name.

BRAINWAVES AND THE LEVEL OF OUR CONSCIOUSNESS

Brainwaves, electrical impulses or neurons in the brain that travel at various speeds and communicate with each other, determine the level of our consciousness. Brainwave speeds are measured in Hertz (cycles per second) and fall into four basic categories: beta (13–38 Hz), alpha (8–13 Hz), theta (4–8 Hz), and delta (0.5–3.5 Hz).

Beta (13–38 Hz) Brainwaves and the World around Us

Beta brainwaves operate when we are wide awake and alert. They fire at rapid speeds and enable us to think on our feet, make rational decisions, solve difficult problems, perform tedious tasks, and remain focused. Our five senses — touch, taste, sight, smell, and hearing — send empirical data to the beta brain, which in turn analyzes and interprets it.[3] Beta waves connect us to the world around us, but they have little or no relationship to paranormal or mystical experiences.

However, alpha, theta, and delta waves, which move at reduced speeds, unlock our psychic potential and open a door to the paranormal. As our brainwaves slow down and the natural world recedes into the background, our faculties are heightened to glimpse the unseen and gain knowledge that seems to be supernatural in origin.

3. When we operate at the beta level for too long, we overload our critical mind and become emotionally stressed and physically drained. We may become irritable and short with colleagues, friends, and family members. Even normal tasks seem to overwhelm us. Therefore, our beta brain needs a break and automatically slows down to the alpha speed, putting us into a semiunconscious state. Our mind begins to wander, our imagination is stimulated, and our focus shifts from the outward world of facts and figures to the inner world of whims and fancies. Once our "batteries" are recharged, we transition back into beta and are ready to tackle the challenges before us.

Most mystical sensations (e.g., ESP, intuitive insight, déjà vu, spontaneous healings, prophetic utterances, spirit messages, automatic writing, and spiritual conversion) occur during the alpha cycle. This likely explains why a majority of people claim at least one psychic experience in their lifetime.

Alpha (8–13 Hz) Brainwaves and the Paranormal

Alpha brainwaves are triggered spontaneously throughout the daylight hours, putting us into semiconscious states. But it is also possible to decrease the speed of brainwaves *at will* through specialized breathing techniques (e.g., eliciting the relaxation response, practicing centering prayer, doing yogic meditation, or undergoing self-hypnosis). In either case, when our brain eases into alpha speed, time seems to slow down and we experience a sense of calmness. Some people report having paranormal experiences, visions, or feelings of being in God's presence. Others claim to receive fresh insights or solutions to long-standing problems. Both Freud and Jung viewed the subconscious as the gateway to creativity.

The subconscious is a repository of wisdom. Herbert Spiegel, MD (1914–2009), an American psychiatrist renowned for his use of therapeutic hypnosis, placed his patients into trance and directed the subconscious mind to solve the particular problem and then reveal it when they came out of trance. This method was highly effective. Milton Erickson, MD, believed everyone possesses an *inward* psychiatrist that can diagnose and treat all manner of problems.

Just how powerful is the subconscious? Here are a few examples of "miraculous" results that can be achieved when individuals enter the alpha brainwave phase.

Alpha and Lamaze

When Lynn became pregnant with our first child, she opted for natural childbirth. At the time, this was not common practice.

"Whoa," I responded. "Is it safe?"

"Yes, and you will be in the delivery room with me."

I shuddered at the thought!

My parents — from a generation when obstetricians anesthetized their patients and delivered babies while the mother was unconscious — thought the idea was preposterous! But Lynn, a graduate of a top-tier nursing program and an operating-room nurse to boot, knew otherwise! Anesthesia can be dangerous.

Lynn told me that she wanted to try the Lamaze method, which utilizes psychoprophylactic means (mental and physical exercises) to lessen painful sensations during labor and delivery. She handed me some brochures that explained the technique. After reading the materials, I was leery. As a fighting fundamentalist and cult buster at the time, I thought Lamaze smacked too much of the New Age philosophy that could open the door to the demonic. But Lynn insisted and asked me to meet Fran, the head nurse of the labor and delivery department and a certified Lamaze instructor, who would be teaching the childbirth classes.

When I explained my concerns, Fran offered that she too was a Christian and the method had no religious connections. It was purely scientific, she said. I was still not convinced but reluctantly agreed to give it a try.

Each week we gathered with other couples in Fran's den. The class began with a few minutes of relaxation exercises. As wives reclined on pillows and the husbands sat behind them, Fran instructed the mothers-to-be to find a focal point on the wall and stare at it continually while breathing rhythmically. About ten minutes into the exercise, she told the husbands to pinch their spouses in a sensitive spot, like on the fleshy back of the upper arm. This was to simulate labor pains. We were all hesitant, at first. But Fran insisted our wives would not feel it. Sure enough, no matter how hard I pinched her, Lynn did not flinch. I was astounded when her arm showed no signs of bruising the next day.

It was not until I studied the subconscious mind years later that I realized how Lamaze works. As Lynn breathed diaphragmatically and concentrated on a focal point, her brain activity shifted from beta to alpha, placing her into a light trance. In this state she felt little or no pain.[4] To us it seemed like a miracle.[5]

Alpha and the Ritual of Snake Handling

Snake handling is one of the more bizarre religious practices in America. It derives from a controversial verse in the Gospel of Mark: "And these signs shall follow them that believe; In my name shall they cast out devils; they shall speak with new tongues. *They shall take up serpents*; and if they drink any deadly thing, it shall not hurt them; they shall lay hands on the sick, and they shall recover" (Mark 16:18 KJV).[6] Based on this text, a small minority of churches in Appalachia literally make it a part of their weekly worship services.

A *typical* snake-handling meeting begins with members of the same sex greeting each other with a holy kiss, followed by spontaneous prayers for God to move among them and give them victory over the serpents. Music accompanies the prayers, and before long, it reaches fever pitch. People weep, wail, sway, shake, and laugh as they call out to Jesus. Some jump up and down like they are bouncing on a trampoline. Others dance "in the Spirit." A few fall to the floor, while others stand with their hands raised up to heaven and their eyes rolled back into their heads. Musicians strum guitars and beat their drums

---

4. Hypnobirthing is another alpha technique some expectant mothers employ to lessen pain during labor and delivery. The method, which involves the use of self-hypnosis, frequently eliminates the need for drugs and shortens the birthing process and postpartum recovery. See Marie Mongan, *Hypnobirthing: A Natural Approach to a Safe, Easier, More Comfortable Birthing* (Palm Beach, FL: HCI, 2015).

5. A similar effect can occur when we are absorbed in a movie. Our brainwaves slow and we forget our pain.

6. See my in-depth article "Snake Handling and Mark 16:18 — Primitive Christianity or Indigenous American Religion," *Criswell Theological Review* 8, no. 1 (Fall 2010): 77–90.

as they lead the congregation in a marathon of singing. Electricity fills the air. One investigator called music the "umbilical cord" of a snake-handling service.[7]

At some point "the anointing" overtakes certain individuals, and they demonstrate it by reaching into the wire cage or wooden box that holds rattlers, copperheads, or cottonmouths. Moving to the syncopation of the music, they lift the serpent high into the air. Both handler and snake seem to writhe in sync.

According to snake handlers, the taking up of serpents is a demonstration of faith. The anointing generates a faith response. In turn, God honors their faithful handling of snakes and protects them.

The anointing is described variously as feeling high, being in God's presence, experiencing joy and peace, getting warm all over, and at times, like being outside one's own body. Sound familiar?

Smithsonian investigator Scott Schwartz theorized that snake handlers slip into an altered state, due to the rhythmic beat of the music and prolonged praying. This enables them effortlessly and calmly — opposite of fight-or-flight — to pick up the vipers.[8]

Another researcher, Tom Burton, received permission to measure the brainwaves of a snake-handling pastor while he was under "the anointing." The EEG (electroencephalogram) revealed that during the course of the meeting the pastor transitioned from beta (13–38 Hz) to alpha (8–13 Hz) and entered a trance-like state.[9]

When their brain activity slows down, people can do amazing things, bordering on the supernatural. The EEG evidence suggests that the ability to pick up poisonous snakes is related as much to brain activity as it is to spirituality. Even on rare occasions when snake han-

7. Mary Lee Daugherty, "Serpent-Handling as Sacrament," *Theology Today* 33, no. 3 (October 1976): 20.

8. Scott Schwartz, *Faith, Serpents, and Fire: Images of Kentucky Holiness Believers* (Jackson: University of Mississippi Press, 1999), 45–47, 60.

9. Thomas Burton, *Serpent-Handling Believers* (Knoxville: University of Tennessee Press, 1993), 139–40.

dlers are bitten, they claim to feel little or no pain — that is, until they move back into the beta state.

Alpha and Healing

Kathryn Kuhlman was a well-known evangelist and healer in the late twentieth century. Her meetings, held in civic auditoriums, drew thousands of seekers. Most arrived hours in advance to find a seat. The worship services included music, a sermon, and "words of knowledge" as Kuhlman called out healings. Selected recipients of healings were ushered to the stage, where Miss Kuhlman briefly interviewed them and then lightly touched their foreheads. Everyone knew what to expect. Overwhelmed by the Spirit, they fell backward, as "catchers" stood behind ready to lower them gently to the floor. A few minutes later they were helped up and returned to their seats.

During my seminary days I attended a Kuhlman rally in Washington, DC, and was moved emotionally by the entire experience. I witnessed people getting out of wheelchairs, casting off body braces, and walking effortlessly across the stage. Kuhlman pronounced cancer victims healed and those with chronic illnesses whole. Shouts of "Praise the Lord" and "Thank you, Jesus" pierced the air. Attendees wept openly and sang spontaneous choruses of *Hallelujah* in unison. Everyone — witnesses and recipients alike — was caught up in the wonderment of the event as it unfolded for three to four hours. I have experienced nothing like it since! I still think back on the scene with great joy and delight. But now, after years of study, I understand some of the psychological dynamics that took place.

The pulsating music, emotional message, dimly lighted arena, swaying bodies, and people being ushered to the stage collectively had an impact on the audience. Caught up in the excitement of the experience, most of the crowd abandoned critical thinking as their brainwaves slowed down significantly, thus making them susceptible to Miss Kuhlman's suggestions and touch. This scientific explanation does not negate the validity of some healings or the reality of their experiences.[10] It simply means the favorable conditions and atmosphere enabled people to believe and receive a healing. Who can say how God works?[11]

Alpha and Hypnosis

Hypnotherapists specialize in placing people into alpha-state trances. Once a client's critical mind recedes, the counselor can impart suggestions to the subconscious mind, like the following:

> "Your eczema is healing and itches less and less."
> "Your warts are dissolving and your skin is clearing up."
> "You are more relaxed at work."
> "You desire to eat healthy foods to improve your health."
> "You are an intuitive thinker, and creative ideas pop into your mind."
> "You feel beautiful and like the way you look."
> "You can look people in the eye and speak with confidence."

10. When Richard Owellen, PhD, MD, a respected scholar, professor, and head of oncology at Johns Hopkins University and Hospital, discovered that his newborn daughter had a congenital hip problem, he was devastated. He consulted with the best specialists, but none offered a solution or even a glimmer of hope. In desperation, he took his daughter to a Kuhlman meeting; she called out the girl's healing. He heard a pop and his daughter's hip rotated back into place.

When I was a young minister in Maryland, I heard that this world-class academic and physician resigned his post at Hopkins to become a pastor of a small "blue-collar" church in Baltimore. He often rented a bus and took people to Kathryn Kuhlman meetings. See Jamie Buckingham, *Daughter of Destiny: The Authorized Biography of Kathryn Kuhlman* (Plainfield, NJ: Logos, 1997), 198.

11. Johnny Carson, host of *The Tonight Show*, invited Kuhlman to be a guest. In the interview, Carson, a self-proclaimed skeptic, asked Kuhlman, "How do you know that most of your healings are not psychosomatic in nature?" She leaned forward and said in essence, "Wouldn't that be wonderful! They come to our service and get healed." Then she fell back into her chair and added, "Most medical professionals say that psychosomatic illnesses are the most difficult to cure." Carson nodded and went to a commercial break.

Suggestions planted in the subconscious mind, if accepted, can manifest themselves when the individual returns to consciousness.[12]

One of the classic case studies of the power of suggestion given to a person while in a hypnotic trance (alpha state) occurred in the late 1700s when Franz Mesmer, the controversial Viennese physician, restored sight to a blind girl. Mesmer incorrectly believed the healing occurred because he was able to manipulate the invisible universal fluids or *heavenly tides* (similar to what the Chinese call *chi*) that flow through the human body. He surmised that too much or too little caused sickness and balance needed to be restored. He sought to adjust these tides through "animal magnetism."[13] In 1784, the king of France appointed a committee to investigate Mesmer's theory and found it lacked a scientific basis. Nearly a half century later, the Academy of Medicine in Paris reopened the investigation and determined that Mesmer's cures were the result of planting suggestions in the minds of his patients, with the body responding accordingly.[14]

12. Gary Elkins, professor of psychology and director of clinical training at Baylor University, has received large research grants from the National Institutes of Health to study the therapeutic use of hypnosis to treat pain for a variety of conditions ranging from menopause to cancer. He has shown quantifiably that hypnotherapy reduces the perception of pain significantly more than a placebo. See R. Alan Streett, "An Interview with Gary Elkins," *Criswell Theological Review* 7, no. 2 (Spring 2010): 49–63.

13. Mesmer's heavenly tide theory is similar to Chinese acupuncture, which teaches that a vibrating energy force called yin and yang (a.k.a. "chi") flows through deep channels in the body called meridians. When there is an imbalance between yin and yang, chaos and disease result. The treatment involves placing needles along the meridians to bring the vital force back into balance and the body back to health. Mesmer, in like fashion, variously used magnets, metal rods, and his hands to cure his patients.

14. The late Ormond McGill, known as the dean of American hypnotists, demonstrated the power of the subconscious when he told a woman in trance that she would be able to hear him speak but not be able to see him. McGill performed a reversal of Mesmer healing a blind girl. View the demonstration at https://www.youtube.com/watch?v=_QrBAGloe2Q.

Alpha and Autosuggestion

Emile Coué (1857–1926), a prominent but controversial French psychologist, hypothesized that imagination is the doorway to the subconscious mind. When we use our imaginations, we automatically slow down our brainwaves, bypass the critical mind, and enter the alpha state. The subconscious mind accepts imaginative thought as being real. It, in turn, motivates the conscious mind to carry out the seemingly impossible. Coué applied his theory mainly to healing diseases. People from across Europe came for cures. Over 200,000 claimed success by using the Coué method, which he called "autosuggestion."[15] He encouraged his patients to close their eyes, get relaxed, and passively repeat twenty times a day in a low voice the formula: "Every day and in every way I am getting better and better." Coué instructed them to imagine their respective diseases being healed. As they repeated the affirmation, their faith grew and results occurred.

Napoleon Hill (1883–1970) applied Coué's principles to finances. His best-selling *Think and Grow Rich* set the standard for all future self-help books.[16] But before he wrote the volume, Hill was a failed and corrupt businessman, driving many businesses into bankruptcy. With its publication he became a millionaire. In *Think and Grow Rich* Hill's philosophy centered on a multiphased application of autosuggestion.[17]

15. See Emile Coué, *Self Mastery through Conscious Autosuggestion* (New York: American Library, 1922).
16. Napoleon Hill, *Think and Grow Rich* (Meriden, CT: Ralston, 1937).
17. They include: (1) create a desire to achieve a goal, (2) demonstrate faith in one's ability to reach the goal, (3) repeat affirmations to strengthen one's resolve and keep focused on the goal, (4) gain knowledge and skills along the way, (5) activate imagination in order to visualize success, (6) map out a strategy to accomplish one's objective, (7) determine to carry out one's plan, (8) strive to persevere and to never give up despite obstacles, (9) seek encouragement from like-minded encouragers, (10) use one's "sexual energy" to drive and sus-

Forty years later, Hill distilled his principles into a single sentence, which he called "the Supreme Secret" of success, when he wrote: "Anything the human mind can believe, the human mind can achieve." Many others have followed in Coué's and Hill's footsteps by combining imagination, faith, and affirmations to achieve various outcomes, whether physical, financial, or psychological. For example, in 2006 Rhonda Byrne's *The Secret* introduced the "Law of Attraction" that states that all goals are attainable by repeating affirmations and believing they will happen.[18] Belief creates expectation; expectation leads to enthusiasm; enthusiasm produces motivation; right attitude attracts the people and the means to achieve one's goals.

Norman Vincent Peale (1898–1993), longtime pastor of Marble Collegiate Church in New York and friend of the rich and famous, touted the *Power of Positive Thinking*, and Robert Schuller (1926–2015), pastor of the Crystal Cathedral in California, labeled his brand of mind over matter "Possibility Thinking."[19] The proponents of the Word of Faith movement call on their adherents to "name it and claim it." Joel Osteen, pastor of the mega Lakewood Church in Houston, Texas, leads his congregation and television viewers in a weekly affirmation. Raising their Bibles high into the air, they all repeat, "This is my Bible. I am what it says, I have what it says I have; I can do what it says I can."

To counter the inhumane treatment of inner-city Blacks in the 1960s and '70s, civil rights leader Jesse Jackson held rallies throughout America in which he called for his followers to repeat aloud after him, "I am somebody." This oft-repeated affirmation instilled in them a sense of self-worth.

---

tain one's resolve, (11) tap into the subconscious mind that empowers the will, (12) employ one's rational mind to carry out one's plans, and (13) trust one's intuition to guide one in decision making in order to reach one's goal.

18. Rhonda Byrne, *The Secret* (New York: Simon & Schuster, 2006).

19. See Norman Vincent Peale, *The Power of Positive Thinking* (New York: Prentice-Hall, 1952), and Robert H. Schuller, *Move Ahead with Possibility Thinking* (New York: Doubleday, 1967).

John Kappas (1925–2002), founder of the Hypnosis Motivation Institute, created the "Mental Bank," a practice of journal keeping in which his clients wrote down daily an affirmation and kept a record of when the affirmation became a reality.[20] He believed documentation of success reinforced the idea that impossible goals can be reached. Autosuggestion is at the core of all these programs and practices. It is not a magic formula or a get-rich-quick scheme, although it is often presented in this way. In fact, most proponents have no inkling of why or how it works.

Autosuggestion is a basic scientific principle: what is implanted in the brain when it operates at alpha speed (8–13 Hz per second) and is accepted by faith has the *potential* to be actualized in time. In the alpha state, the subconscious mind absorbs the positive suggestions and then stimulates and aids the conscious mind (at beta speed) to discover ways and means to accomplish the desired goals.[21]

Alpha and Automatic Writing

Psychics tout automatic writing as the ability to receive and transcribe messages from the spirit world. It would be better to see it as originating from the subconscious mind during the alpha state.

Arthur Conan Doyle, creator of the Sherlock Holmes mysteries and a respected medical doctor in England during the late nineteenth and early twentieth centuries, promoted psychic causes, especially spiritualism (communication with the dead). His wife claimed the ability to receive messages from beyond the grave through the means of automatic writing. Doyle was a personal friend of magician Harry Houdini, a psychic debunker. Never was there an odder friendship —

20. John G. Kappas, *Success Is Not an Accident: The Mental Bank Concept* (Tarzana, CA: Panorama, 1987).

21. In other words, positive affirmations work only when supported by accompanying actions. In many ways it differs little from goal setting and finding ways and means to effectuate the desired outcome.

the confirmed believer and the skeptic. In an effort to convince Houdini of spiritualism, Doyle invited him to sit with Mrs. Doyle and allow her to contact Houdini's dead mother. As Mrs. Doyle picked up the pen, her hand moved across the paper and a message was received. Harry knew immediately the communication was not from his sainted mother. First, the message was written in English. His mother spoke only Yiddish. Second, she addressed him as Harry (his stage name). In life, she always called him Erich (his birth name). Mrs. Doyle sincerely believed she had made contact, but the message actually came from her subconscious mind.

Another proponent of automatic writing was Rosemary Isabel Brown (1916–2001), a British housewife and novice piano player with little talent, who wrote hundreds of musical pieces that she claimed were channeled to her psychically by the world's greatest dead composers, including Franz Liszt, Franz Schubert, Frédéric Chopin, Johann Sebastian Bach, Johannes Brahms, and Ludwig van Beethoven, among others.[22] She transcribed the works through automatic writing, and each reflected the unique style of the composer. Musicologists, psychologists, and investigative reporters have studied Brown's compositions, concluding that most of her works are classics, if not masterpieces. Many concert pianists have performed her works in live performances.

Although Rosemary Brown attributed her musical achievements to contact with past masters, John Anthony Sloboda, research professor at Guildhall School of Music and Drama (London), more accurately characterized Ms. Brown's accomplishments as "the most convincing case of unconscious composition on a large scale."[23] The power of the brain operating at alpha speed can produce extraordinary effects!

---

22. See Rosemary Brown, *Unfinished Symphonies: Voices from the Beyond* (New York: Morrow, 1971).

23. Quoted by Matthew Brown, *Debussy Redux: The Impact of His Music on Popular Culture* (Bloomington: Indiana University Press, 2012), 36–37.

Alpha and Reincarnation

Reincarnation is a belief that upon physical death the soul continues to live and takes up residence in another body. Many claim to have lived on earth many times throughout history.[24] Most researchers attribute memories of past incarnations to cryptomnesis, a theory that people may recall forgotten memories but believe they are new or original.[25] These restored memories often surface during past life regression sessions under hypnosis when the subject is in an alpha state. The classic example is the case for Bridey Murphy.

Businessman Morey Bernstein (1919–1999) of Pueblo, Colorado, was also an amateur hypnotist. When he placed his neighbor Virginia Tighe into a trance and regressed her back to childhood, he hoped she could recover some childhood memories. On one occasion she jumped back in time before her birth and began to speak with an Irish brogue. She identified herself as Bridey Murphy from Cork, Ireland, and proceeded to give details of her life, death in 1864, and subsequent reincarnation in 1923. Bernstein did only minimal research to confirm the revelations but believed in his heart they were accurate. This led to a best-selling book (and later a movie) called *The Search for Bridey Murphy*.[26] Bernstein included quotes from Jesus to bolster his case.[27]

---

24. While in a trance, Edgar Cayce spoke of the reality of reincarnation and claimed to have lived before. However, in his waking state he doubted its veracity. Ted Swager did the same.

25. Ian Stevenson, MD (1918–2007), was an exception. A research professor at the University of Virginia School of Medicine, Stevenson devoted much of his academic career to the study of reincarnation and authored fourteen books on the subject, including *Twenty Cases of Reincarnation* (Charlottesville: University of Virginia Press, 1966).

26. Morey Bernstein, *The Search for Bridey Murphy* (Garden City, NY: Doubleday, 1956).

27. He quoted Jesus saying, "Unless one is born again, he cannot see the kingdom of God" and "You must be born again" (John 3:3, 8); "And if you are willing to accept what I say, he [John the Baptist] is Elijah, the one the prophets said would come" (Matt. 11:14); "Rabbi, who sinned, this man or his parents,

In my early days of searching for spiritual reality, I read it with great interest and thought reincarnation might be a possibility.

It was later discovered that Virginia Tighe's parents were part Irish and that Bridey Murphy Corkell, an Irish immigrant, lived across the street from her childhood home. This was the likely source of information Virginia recalled from her subconscious mind under hypnosis.

Alpha and Divine Encounters

The book of Acts tells how Peter, a rambunctious follower of Jesus, went up to a rooftop in Joppa to pray and "fell into a *trance*" (Acts 10:10). In this altered state he saw heaven open and something like a large sheet coming down and being lowered to the ground by its four corners. In it were all kinds of four-footed creatures and reptiles and birds of the air. He then heard a voice saying, "Get up, Peter; kill and eat." But Peter replied, "By no means, Lord; for I have never eaten anything that is profane or unclean." The voice said to him again, a second time, "What God has made clean, you must not call profane." This happened three times, and the sheet was suddenly taken up to heaven (vv. 10–15).

This was a spontaneous and private experience. One doubts that Mrs. Peter would have seen the sheet or heard the voice had she visited the roof. Peter alone had an encounter with God during his trance.

The apostle Paul, likewise, unexpectedly slipped into an altered state when praying during a visit to the temple. He tells of the event:

> "After I had returned to Jerusalem and while I was praying in the temple, I fell into a *trance* and saw Jesus saying to me, 'Hurry and get out of Jerusalem quickly, because they will not accept your testimony about me.' And I said, 'Lord, they themselves know that in every synagogue I imprisoned and beat those who believed in you.

---

that he was born blind?" (John 9:2). How could the man have sinned before he was born? According to Bernstein, the man must have lived before.

And while the blood of your witness Stephen was shed, I myself was standing by, approving and keeping the coats of those who killed him.' Then he said to me, 'Go, for I will send you far away to the Gentiles.'" (Acts 22:17–21)

This transcendental encounter was a confirmation of an earlier call Paul had on the Damascus road when his horse reared and threw him to the ground. At the time, Paul was on a mission to search out Christ followers and haul them to jail. As he looked up from the dust, he saw and heard the heavenly Jesus. None of Paul's traveling companions experienced the vision. Only Paul!

The apostle John, while exiled on the Isle of Patmos for preaching the gospel, suddenly found himself "in the spirit" (Rev. 1:10; 4:2; 17:3; 21:10) on the Lord's Day, and he had a visionary encounter with Christ, followed by an angelic tour of heaven. Although John's feet were firmly planted on the ground, he found himself standing before the throne of God.

In more modern times, Marcus Borg (1942–2015), a well-known and influential New Testament scholar, tells of having several numinous experiences. The first happened as he drove through the snow-covered Minnesota countryside. He had been on the road for about three hours with the drone of the car engine his only companion. Suddenly everything changed — the trees, the fields, the paved highway, and even Borg himself were encased in a bright yellow light. Everything glowed. In this altered state of consciousness, Borg felt connected to everything around him. This sense of union or oneness with the divine lasted only sixty seconds or so, but it profoundly changed his understanding of God and nature. He later described this transcendent encounter as "the richest minute of my life."[28]

Over the next years, Borg had more prolonged experiences. "A few were triggered by music"[29] as he listened to a chamber orchestra during

---

28. Marcus Borg, *Convictions* (New York, HarperOne, 2014), 37.
29. Borg, *Convictions*, 37.

a college chapel service and while he attended a symphony in a concert hall. In his midfifties, while on a flight to Tel Aviv, Borg slipped into a trance that lasted for about forty minutes. Everything and everyone around him looked beautiful and glowed. He remembered how he wanted to remain in this state of euphoria forever but was jarred back to consciousness when the flight attendant clanged dishes as she cleaned up after supper. The afterglow lasted for several more minutes.[30]

In each instance Borg sensed God's manifest presence and all-encompassing love. As a result, Borg's understanding of God expanded and he embraced *panentheism*, a belief that all of creation is enveloped in God; yet God is more than the sum total of creation (Ps. 139:7–10; Acts 17:27–28).[31] Panentheism combines both the *transcendence* and *immanence* of God (1 Kings 8:27).[32]

Not all encounters with the divine occur spontaneously. Some are intentionally self-induced. LSD[33] and other hallucinogenic drugs such as "sacred" or magical mushrooms have a propensity to biologically produce inner "spiritual" experiences ranging from euphoria to monstrous hallucinations.[34] Some Native American tribes use peyote to tap into the world beyond and gain spiritual insights. To Rastafarians, smoking cannabis is a sacrament, and, when combined with prayer, some believe that they can commune with their inner divinity or the spirit of Haile Selassie. In his book *The Art of Spiritual Hypnosis: Ac-*

---

30. Borg, *Convictions*, 37–38.

31. Borg, *Convictions*, 45. Others, however, who have had similar experiences as Borg's, continue to embrace traditional Christian monotheism.

32. Borg, *Convictions*, 47.

33. In the 1960s and '70s, Harvard psychologist Timothy Leary introduced LSD as a means to explore inner reality and called on students to "Tune in, turn on, and drop out." A drug-induced counterculture movement was born.

34. In 2006 researchers at Johns Hopkins Center for Psychedelic and Consciousness Research produced a landmark double-blind study of the benefits of psychedelics and how they produce spiritual incidents similar to spontaneously occurring mystical experiences. See R. R. Griffiths et al., "Psilocybin Can Occasion Mystical-Type Experiences Having Substantial and Sustained Personal Meaning and Spiritual Significance," *Psychopharmacology* 187 (2006): 268–83.

cessing Divine Wisdom, Roy Hunter, a well-respected hypnotherapist, relates how scores of clients from a variety of religious backgrounds have had transformative encounters with God while hypnotized.[35]

Church history is replete with examples of Christ followers who sought divine visitations, visions and heavenly encounters through the practice of spiritual disciplines. The desert fathers, third-century mystics, formed monastic communities composed of like-minded priests who practiced a prayer tradition known as *hesychasm* (Greek, meaning stillness and rest). It involved emptying the mind through meditation and silent repetition of the Jesus Prayer in order to attain mystical union with God.

During the Middle Ages, a wider revival of mysticism occurred under Meister Eckhart (ca. 1260–1328), Catherine of Siena (1347–1380), Thomas à Kempis (1380–1471), and Teresa of Ávila (1515–1582). In her book *The Interior Castle*, Teresa describes her search for intimate union with the divine as an inward journey achieved through contemplative prayer, asceticism, and devotion.[36] She depicts the "Interior Castle" as seven "mansions" that she must pass through to get closer to God. Teresa's seven-step process, while couched in Christian terms, looks very similar to the path of kabbalah and the seven chakras of Hinduism.[37]

✦

Whether spontaneous or sought after, varieties of mystical experiences have one thing in common. From a biological standpoint, they all occur when our brainwaves slow to the alpha rate of 8–13 Hz, resulting in altered states of consciousness (ASC). As functional magnetic res-

35. Roy Hunter, *The Art of Spiritual Hypnosis: Accessing Divine Wisdom* (New York: Blooming Twigg, 2016).

36. Reprint editions of the book are now available from many publishers.

37. People from all religious backgrounds — Shintoists, Sufis, kabbalists, Catholic mystics, Buddhists, Hindus, evangelical Christians — have so-called encounters with the divine. Mystical experiences, even the "spiritual" ones, do not constitute salvation.

onance imaging (fMRI) shows conclusively, specific parts of our brain light up when we enter an ASC. How we interpret the experience, though, depends on our belief system.[38]

While the majority of our memorable mystical events and feelings take place during waking hours, the deepest and most vivid ones transpire while we sleep, as our brainwaves slow down even more to the theta (4–8 Hz) and delta (0.5–3.5 Hz) cycles.

38. See William James, *Varieties of Religious Experience* (New York: Penguin, 1985). Regardless of our particular mystical experiences (e.g., tongues, trances, being slain in the Spirit, out-of-body travel), they are produced by the brain.

17

NIGHTTIME BRAINWAVES
AND PSYCHIC PHENOMENA

Our most intense and dramatic psychic experiences and otherworldly encounters happen while we sleep; for most of us,
that is between approximately 10 p.m. and 6 a.m. Our brain slows
down to theta speed (4–8 Hz) as we fall asleep at night and remains
there for a few minutes before slowing down even more to delta
speed (0.5–3.5 Hz). In the morning, as we emerge from sleep, the
brain speed increases to theta once again but remains there for only
a few minutes.

THETA AND THE SUPERNATURAL

Of all the brainwave categories, theta is by far the shortest in dura-
tion. In this groggy, momentary twilight period — between deep sleep
and waking up — we are most susceptible to intense hallucinations,
encounters with angels and demons, and even so-called alien abductions, any of which can leave us confused and frightened.

Theta and Visitations

One morning I received a frantic phone call from my dad saying he had a horrific experience that left him shaken and disoriented. He told me that when he awakened and opened his eyes, he saw a demon sitting on his chest attempting to strangle the life out of him. My father was helpless; he couldn't move, breathe, or speak. Finally, in desperation, he managed to call out, "Jesus, help me!" The demon fled immediately!

We talked for a long time and concluded that a demon tried to kill my father. But why? We didn't know.

I, too, had a somewhat similar, but less scary, experience while attending seminary. I participated in a late-night prayer meeting when a fellow seminarian named Tom suddenly began to speak in unknown "tongues." The meeting continued past 2 a.m. I returned to my dorm room exhausted and hopped immediately into bed. As I was about to doze off, I sensed a presence in the room and looked up to see a hideous impish figure standing in the darkened corner. Sneering and laughing, it mockingly announced, "Tom is ours. We won't let him go."

For many years, whenever I spoke about the reality of demons, I told and retold these stories. I often asked my listeners if any of them had ever had a comparable experience. I was always surprised at the number of people who raised their hands.

In my later years, as I studied the effects of brainwave scans, I discovered a *natural* or scientific explanation for these bedtime and predawn experiences. During these brief transitory theta states (when we are on the cusp of entering and coming out of sleep), we can suffer "sleep paralysis," also known as hypnagogic hallucinations, a condition characterized by a sense that some strange entity or otherworldly personage is present in our room. Between 25 and 40 percent of all people have these experiences. Occasionally, these seemingly hideous beings attempt to choke us or exert pressure on our chest. Unable to move or speak, the sleeper panics. After several seconds, as the brainwaves increase in speed, the person is able to react verbally. In my father's case, he cried out, "Jesus, help me!"

Because sleep paralysis occurs naturally, it subsides on its own as we become more conscious. The cry for help is irrelevant. My dad could have called out for Eleanor Roosevelt or Donald Duck to save him and gotten the same result.

Since the beginning of recorded history people have told and retold stories of similar attacks and visitations at bedtime and upon rising. The form and nature of the perceived phantoms are dependent on the particular culture and myths at the time. They have included visitations from vampires, werewolves, witches (known as "old hags"), aliens, and spirits — both good and bad.

Theta and Floating

Another phenomenon associated with theta brainwaves is a sense of floating upward. This experience may be interpreted in one of several ways.

In a letter to the Corinthian church, Saint Paul tells of being "caught up" or ascending to the third heaven, where he heard words so sacred that he dared not repeat them (2 Cor. 12:1–4). While he does not mention the exact time of day that his divine encounter occurred, entering or exiting the theta state provides a viable frame of reference.

Harriet Tubman, the runaway slave and abolition leader, had numerous floating experiences. While laboring in the fields, she often collapsed and fell unconscious. In the brief moments of going into or coming out of seizures, she says she floated above the earth and watched as people below surrounded her limp body. The floating was regularly accompanied by visions of freedom, which she interpreted as signs that God wanted her to free the people. Tubman called these episodes her "sleeping spells."[1]

---

1. Nicole London, *Harriet Tubman: Visions of Freedom*, video (Owings Mills, MD: Maryland Public Television, 2022).

A neighbor once told me that every afternoon she struggled to stay awake. Despite exhaustion, she strove to remain conscious because she had three toddlers at home and feared for their safety. One day as she lay on the sofa, her eyes closed and suddenly her soul floated upward to the ceiling. From this vantage point she continued to watch her children as they played together. She felt comforted that she could both sleep and keep an eye on the kids.

Knowing that I was a minister, she sought my opinion. Based on my fundamentalist theology and lack of understanding of mind-body science at the time, I gave her less than wise advice. I attributed her experience to demonic activity! The young mother was terrified! Only years later did I learn about floating and the theta state. On the positive side, fearing the worst, my neighbor never again fell asleep during the day or neglected her children!

Others have reported out-of-body experiences during surgery in which they observed the operation from above. These likely happen as anesthesia wears off and the patient is about to wake up. Some floating cases are also associated with so-called alien abductions and can be quite frightening. They often follow a common pattern. A person is asleep face up and suddenly encounters an eerie creature or feels a strange hovering presence. Paralyzed and unable to move, the victim floats upward. Upon awakening, these persons cannot remember what happened. Filled with anxiety and plagued by dark fears, they seek answers from a hypnotist who mentally regresses them and enables them to recall the details — how they floated up to a spacecraft, encountered aliens who communicated through telepathy, examined them, and returned them to earth. Their ascension was actually a theta-induced hypnagogic hallucination and not an alien abduction.

Many sects teach their followers to practice astral projection, the intentional separation of soul from body.[2] When successful, the freed

2. Eckankar, the "ancient science of soul travel," teaches that astral projection is the path to salvation. Once the soul is liberated from the physical body, it is free to ascend to the various spiritual planes of existence until it reaches

soul can travel to heavenly realms and contact ascended masters who offer spiritual enlightenment and a path to salvation. Many ECK members claim they have made the trip. In reality, their floating experiences are brain related and take place during theta sleep.

In my early days in spiritualism, I followed Arthur Ford's step-by-step instructions on separating body and soul. He suggested that aspiring trance mediums should lie down, meditate, and breathe rhythmically, so that the soul can propel out of the body. This provides an open door for a spirit guide to take up residence. I regularly practiced this discipline. One night as I lay supine and breathed deeply, my spine vibrated violently and it seemed my soul struggled to be free. I began to panic and cried out to God for help before I collapsed into a deep sleep.

Only years later did I come to understand my experience as a naturally produced theta phenomenon.

Theta and Sex

Even more bizarre is the account of Elisabeth Kübler-Ross (1926–2004), the famous psychiatrist and author of the best-selling book *On Death and Dying* who was the first to identify the five stages of grief.[3] Her professional interest in mortality led her to explore and adopt some strange theories and practices. In the late 1970s, she studied out-of-body experiences and spiritualism as a possible means of contacting the deceased. Her study of ancient cultures and their understanding of postdeath experiences led her to believe that the spirit of a departed loved one — known as *incubus* (male) and *succubus* (female) — could truly visit the living in order to have phantasmic sex with them as they slept.[4]

Sugmad, the ECK version of God. For more information on the occult roots of Eckankar and its founder Paul Twitchell, see Brad Steiger, *In My Soul I Am Free* (Crystal, MN: Illuminated Way, 1968).

3. See Elisabeth Kübler-Ross, *On Death & Dying* (New York: Simon & Schuster, 1969).

4. For a short time, Kübler-Ross aligned with the teachings of Jay Barham,

Accounts of nocturnal visits date back four thousand years to Mesopotamia and continue into the present. The term "incubus" comes from the Latin *incubo*, meaning "nightmare." According to legend, Merlin the magician, who appears in the tales of King Arthur, was conceived through the union of an incubus and a maiden. Such folklore was likely an attempt to explain natural nocturnal occurrences, namely, wet dreams and night terrors, all associated with hypnagogic paralysis and experienced at the theta level of consciousness.

DELTA AND PROPHETIC INSIGHT

When our brainwaves at night reach their slowest range (delta, 0.5–3.5 Hz), we fall into deep sleep, are unconscious of our surroundings, and do not respond to normal physical cues. Someone can call our name or cry "fire," and we will not budge. One phase of delta, known as REM (rapid eye movement) sleep, is associated mainly with dreams, although it has many other functions. Our first of four rounds of REM starts about ten minutes after we fall asleep, and others occur approximately every two hours thereafter.

Delta and Dreams

While we sleep, we process the previous day's events and experiences through metaphorical dreams. Our brain stores information from some dreams for future reference and expunges the rest as unimportant. Interestingly, according to some Native American traditions, dreams — both good and bad — fill the night air. To filter the positive from the negative, they hang a dream catcher over their beds. Good

---

founder of the Church of the Facet of the Divinity, who claimed he was a channel for incubi and succubi. A thorough investigation uncovered that Barham himself was the nightly specter who visited vulnerable church members. When he was exposed as a psychic fraud and con artist, Kübler-Ross initially refused to believe the accusations, but she finally renounced the cult-like leader in 1981.

dreams pass through outer holes and slide down the soft feathers of the catcher. Bad dreams get entangled and dissolve with the rising of the sunlight. This may not be a scientific fact, but the idea reflects truth. Dreams have meaning and purpose.

Some dreams are prophetic and motivate the dreamer to act once awake. Ancient Israelites viewed these night visions as inspired. As Moses, Aaron, and Miriam stood before the entrance to the tabernacle, God spoke:

> "When there are prophets among you,
>   I the LORD make myself known to them in visions;
>   I speak to them in dreams." (Num. 12:6)[5]

God's people, however, were not the only ones to have prophetic dreams and visions. In the book of Daniel, Nebuchadnezzar, a pagan king, had a series of dreams but was unable to discern their meaning or significance. The prophet Daniel, recognizing their divine origin, gave the interpretation (Dan. 2:24–45).

On the day of Pentecost, the apostle Peter declared from the portico of the temple,

> "Your sons and your daughters shall prophesy,
>   and your young men shall see visions,
>   and your old men shall dream dreams." (Acts 2:17)

The divine means of communication surpassed the critical mind and occurred at the subconscious level.

Another case is found in the book of Acts when the apostle Paul and his team interpreted a symbolic dream to mean that God wanted them to carry the message of Christ westward to the continent of Europe rather than eastward into the Orient (Acts 16:9).

---

5. Joseph, Samuel, Isaiah, Ezekiel, Elijah, Jeremiah, and Daniel were some of the other prophets to whom God spoke through dreams.

The well-known psychiatrist Carl Jung, the son of a Swiss Reformed pastor, believed we encounter God in dreams and receive divine guidance.[6] Freud, on the other hand, called dreams "the royal road to the unconscious." He saw them as the way our repressed ego displays its deep-seated desires. As a result, he encouraged his patients to probe the meaning of their dreams; hence, some psychotherapists suggest that patients keep dream journals.

Delta and Healing

Our body has built-in mechanisms to fight potential illnesses and to remedy physical problems when something goes awry. It is during deep sleep, especially during REM sleep, that our body restores itself and the immune system is strengthened.[7] The ancient Greeks believed dreams possessed therapeutic properties.[8]

Ironically, one of the worst settings for sleep is a hospital. Because of numerous interruptions, the circadian rhythm is disturbed, and as a result, very little sleep occurs and dreams are rare. The place where healing is supposed to take place can actually be a hindrance to the immune system. Best to keep our hospital stays short.

For much of history, humans did not have the advantage of modern medicine. Survival depended solely on the power of the inner physician — the immune system — to heal and repair.

6. Paul Meier and Robert Wise, *Windows of the Soul: A Look at Dreams and Their Meanings* (Nashville: Nelson, 1995), 109–10, 157–58. Also see Ronald Hayman, *A Life of Jung* (New York: Norton, 1999), 231.

7. If, however we continually abuse our bodies and our health deteriorates as a result, the overworked immune system may not be able to restore us to wholeness. Additionally, when we fall victim to an accident or face a major health crisis, we often need the help of a physician or surgeon to set bones, remove diseased organs, and sew up lacerations. Even then, our body must take over and complete the healing process.

8. In the cult of Asclepius, the god of medicine and healing, members practiced incubation rituals designed to initiate sacred dreams and activate healing.

Delta and Problem Solving

We have all heard or repeated the aphorism "I need to sleep on it." What we mean is that a problem is too complex to solve immediately in our current state of mind. More time and further consideration are needed. According to scientists, the idiom conveys a literal truth. At night, as our brain slows to delta speed, we are often able to solve difficult challenges that eluded us in our waking hours.[9] On occasion I have come up one word short on a difficult *New York Times* crossword puzzle, only to wake in the middle of the night with the answer.

Several years ago, I purchased a set of Christmas tree lights. When I opened the box, I realized I was in trouble. The string of lights was multifaceted with three different strands that were all connected in the middle. No matter how hard I tried, I was unable to figure out how to hang the crazy things. My entire family joined me, to no avail. We must have wasted two or three hours. The lights were an enigma. I decided to return them to the store the next day, but at 3 a.m. my unconscious mind processed and figured out the problem. Voilà!

In *Lectures to My Students*, Charles Spurgeon, arguably the nineteenth century's greatest preacher, tells how one Saturday evening he was unable to grasp his biblical text or put together a cogent sermon outline. He went to bed without any idea what he would preach the next morning. But while he slept it all coalesced. He woke, grabbed a candle and a notepad, wrote down everything, and then went back to bed and slept like a baby. Spurgeon claimed it was one of the best sermons he ever preached!

Dreams have been the source of great works of art, music, novels, films, mathematical proofs, scientific discoveries, and sundry inventions. Here are a few of the examples.

9. For a medically sound yet commonsense approach for understanding the nature of dreams and interpreting them, see Meier and Wise, *Windows of the Soul*, 63–85.

Elias Howe (1819–1867), inventor of the modern sewing machine, was stymied when it came to the special kind of needle required for his machine to operate flawlessly. He decided to sleep on it. In a dream, he encountered a group of cannibals that threatened to kill and eat him if he could not design the needle. The dream ended with his death as the cannibals stabbed him with spears having holes in their tips. When he awoke, his problem was solved. He placed a hole in the end of the needle, and the sewing machine was born.

Niels Bohr (1885–1962), the father of quantum mechanics, was at a standstill in his attempt to discern the structure of an atom. One night he dreamed about atoms and suddenly saw the nucleus of the atom and electrons spinning around it similar to planets spinning around the sun. The next morning, he entered his lab and tested his visionary hypothesis, which proved true. He was later awarded the Nobel Prize for Physics for the discovery.

Jack Nicklaus, perhaps the greatest golfer of all time, was in a slump. His drives and iron shots were missing the mark. One night he dreamed of playing an amazing round of golf. Looking down at his grip, he noticed the position of his hands on the club. The next morning, he adopted the grip he saw in his dream. His slump ended.

Steve Allen (1921–2000) was an American television and radio personality, comedian, musician, composer, author, and actor. In 1954, he cocreated and hosted *The Tonight Show*, the first late-night talk show to air on television. But he will be best remembered for writing the opening song for the musical *The Bachelor* (1956). He labored for days to write the lyrics but drew a blank. Facing a hard deadline, he instructed his subconscious mind before he hopped in bed to write a smash hit. The lyrics came in a dream, and the next morning he jotted down the words: "This could be the start of something big." Nearly every major soloist has recorded it.

The power of the brain in the delta dream state is phenomenal![10]

10. Stories abound of the power of dreams. Robert Louis Stevenson said his dreams provided him with some of the best plots for his stories. Coleridge wrote

SUMMARY

During the daytime hours our beta brainwaves fire at top speed and we are fully conscious and able to deal with matters that require rational thinking and critical analysis. Beta is the realm of the *normal*. But unusual things happen when the brain slows to alpha and we enter an altered state of consciousness. We see mental images, hear sounds not discernible to the ear, get intuitive insights, and have psychic impulses. Theta and delta brainwaves operate as we sleep. In these unconscious states we may have paranormal experiences, including strange and bizarre encounters with demons and angels, prophetic utterances, creative problem solving, and even healing of the body. The subconscious mind is a storehouse of untapped resources and wisdom that can transform our dreams into reality.

---

his famous poem *Kubla Khan* as a result of an opium-influenced dream. In 1869, Russian chemist Dmitri Mendeleev developed the periodic table of elements as a result of a dream. He claimed he saw a table with all the chemical elements arranged according to their atomic weight.

18

Searching for Ted Swager

I now understood that while psychic experiences varied (e.g., automatic writing, intuition, angelic encounters, speaking to spirits, prophetic and inspired words, or spontaneous healing), they all had a common source — the subconscious mind, or more specifically, our brain as it operates at different speeds.

As I neared the end of my quest to discover the source and nature of the paranormal, I wanted to reconnect with Ted Swager to share my latest discoveries with him and compare notes. It was now 2014, and we had lost touch. Since my last contact with him, eighteen years had flown by. I Googled him and came up empty-handed, except for a few old newspaper clippings. Ted had no social media footprint — no Facebook, Twitter, LinkedIn, or Instagram. Nothing!

I found no obituary for him; so, I knew he was alive. If our last correspondence was any indication, he was not in the best of health. I kept searching for him, believing our relationship needed some closure.

Then one day, I came across a chat-room discussion and found two long posts written by a woman identified only as "Anna" in which she tells of consulting Ted a few years earlier. Maybe Anna could provide me with a clue into Ted's whereabouts and current activities. She begins by mentioning Ted's past association with Arthur Ford and the Spiritual Frontiers Fellowship and describes Ted as "a superb Jungian analyst."[1]

Anna sought Ted's counsel because she was plagued by horrific nightmares, which often jolted her out of sleep at night and caused a deep sense of dread throughout the day, which she could not shake off. Ted suggested she write her dreams in a journal, which they discussed at each visit. She said Ted believed her dark dreams were symptomatic of an "inner turmoil" caused by some outside activity or relationship.

In her first counseling session, Anna mentioned to Ted that she had been reading and following the teachings of the Hermetic Order of the Golden Dawn, an occult society that promotes communication with ascended masters and spirits of the dead. Ted advised her to cease immediately, saying she had opened a "Pandora's box" that led to the bizarre and eerie phantoms that appeared in her dreams.

I found the post encouraging. Ted no longer practiced spiritualism. He had even discouraged Anna from exploring contact with celestial beings and spirits of the dead. From my perspective, this was good news.

I also learned that Anna was a resident of Washington, DC, and traveled three times a week to southern Maryland to meet with Ted. Her posts noted that Ted's fees were substantial, but she willingly paid them because he offered her "a safe environment," at least temporarily. "For a few hours a week," she writes, "I was able to get away from the chaotic and confused political life of Washington."

I wondered about Anna's connection to Washington politics. Was she a Georgetown lady? Did she work at the Pentagon or State Department? Or might she be the spouse of a high-ranking official or

---

1. Jung believed the subconscious mind held the clue to understanding one's thoughts and behaviors. He also believed that the subconscious mind reveals itself in universal archetypes, which are universal patterns and symbols that signify meaning. They manifest themselves in dreams and phobias, which can be interpreted by a trained therapist.

bureaucrat? Whatever the answer, she was under pressure and possibly in danger, and turned to Ted Swager for help. He provided the "safe environment." I was amazed that Ted, after so many years, still had contacts with the Washington political set.

Further along in the post, Anna mentions that Ted probed her subconscious mind and offered wisdom from his own. This is how she understood the sessions. According to Anna, Ted's sage advice came from his subconscious and reached into hers. This was in line with her earlier observation that Ted was a "Jungian analyst." She also calls Ted a "true Sufi," that is, one whose life manifests light, knowledge, and wisdom. Anna concludes her post by saying she was extremely satisfied with the outcome of her counseling sessions.

I tried by every means to contact Anna but hit a dead end.

Anna's two chat-room posts were the only information I had on Ted, until a Google alert arrived in my email linking to his obituary.

♦

Ted Swager passed away on March 10, 2015, at the Genesis Nursing Home in Annapolis, Maryland. He was eighty-four years old. The death notice mentioned that besides his counseling ministry Ted had pastored in Maryland, Delaware, Pennsylvania, Tennessee, and Maine. Lois, the love of his life, who served as his moral compass, preceded him in death in 2009.

Before graduating from Wesley Theological Seminary and entering the ministry, Ted taught high school and coached football in a small town in western Pennsylvania.

The obituary provided me with the names of Ted's surviving adult sons. I was able to contact two of the three through email. One was not interested in speaking with me and was somewhat hostile. He felt many people took advantage of his dad, and he was angry. The other son, Bill — a professional trumpeter and music store owner — was more cordial. A devout Christian, he expressed regret for his father's occult adventures and thought they were misguided. I offered no personal opinion but told him I had known his dad since the late 1960s, to which he responded, "Yes, I remember him mentioning you often as one of the good guys." I hoped that meant Ted considered me a kindred spirit, as I did him. In passing, Bill said he had some of his father's papers and sermons stored away that likely included information on Ted's years in spiritualism. I thought about asking permission to look through them but didn't want to seem brazen. We exchanged a few emails, but Bill soon stopped writing and no longer responded to my emails. He was busy or likely thought of me as some kind of curiosity seeker, fringe character, or kook — or all the above! Then in January 2022, I received another Google alert, this time informing me that Bill Swager had unexpectedly passed away at the age of sixty-nine. Ted Swager's legacy was quickly fading with time.

✦

Some wise but anonymous soul once said, "Everyone dies twice. Once when you stop breathing and a second time, a bit later, when somebody mentions your name on earth for the last time."[2]

I am one of the few who still remembers Ted and his accomplishments. I regret I did not reply to his last letter or simply hop on a plane to meet with him when I had the chance. In the end we had both landed on the same page, believing psychic manifestations are products of the subconscious mind. Ted came to this conclusion after he left spiritualism and rejected the theory that ESP is demonic in nature. His findings were based on his own experiences and common sense. I took a more circuitous route, which entailed fifty years of research into magic, mentalism, and the mind-body connection.[3]

2. This quote has been attributed to an anonymous graffiti artist from Bristol, England, who calls himself Banksy. His true identity is unknown.

3. I now remembered what Ted told Dr. Pyke and me in our "intervention session" with him, that he now believed his psychic abilities came from his subconscious and not "the other side." Dr. Pyke and I had dismissed this explanation and written him off as a scammer. In truth, Ted knew back then what I was just learning. I now wished I had listened.

Ted Swager was my friend. He dedicated his life to serving others. He never abandoned his faith and always encouraged clients, family, and friends to follow Jesus Christ and his precepts, particularly to love one another. I hope this book will help Ted Swager's name to live a little longer.

19

Lessons Learned

O ver the past half century, I have attended séances, psychic events, and lectures, and have read hundreds of books on spiritualism, ESP, and the paranormal from historical, spiritual, and psychological perspectives. I have both advocated for and preached against parapsychology.

Each new encounter and experience caused me to reevaluate my previous understanding of psychic and spiritual phenomena.

Stage 1. Influenced by the Spiritual Frontiers Fellowship, I initially believed that modern-day psychic gifts and paranormal manifestations were identical to the spiritual gifts and miracles found in the Bible. Additionally, I believed that trance mediums were able to communicate with the dead. That was where my journey began.

Stage 2. After my dramatic conversion, I came under the influence of prominent fundamentalist leaders who believed that all psychic manifestations were demonic counterfeits of biblical miracles intended to deceive the masses. People needed to be warned. To this end, I became an evangelist, apologist, and psychic debunker.

Stage 3. When I discovered the inner workings of mentalism (a branch of professional magic), I began to question the demonic-origin theory and concluded that most psychics were merely clever fakers who used trickery to dupe the gullible and profit financially.

Stage 4. On the latest leg of my journey, I discovered the power of the subconscious mind. When our brainwaves slow and our consciousness is altered, we can have a variety of mystical experiences that border on the paranormal. The brain is powerful and capable of producing incredible phenomena.

Based on my personal experiences, academic research, and overall cumulative knowledge, I am now ready to draw a few conclusions for your consideration and tell you where my research is now leading me.

On the Matter of Psychic versus Spiritual Manifestations

It is nearly impossible to discern the difference between psychic and spiritual gifts. According to biblical accounts, Jesus and his disciples healed people, encountered angels and demons, spoke to the dead, and functioned in the realm of signs and wonders. Modern-day psychics and mystics, especially those claiming to be Christians, believe their experiences are similar in nature. They see no difference. Edgar Cayce was a lifelong Disciples of Christ Sunday school teacher, Olga Worrall was the daughter of a Russian Orthodox theology professor, and Ted Swager was an ordained Methodist clergyman. They each claimed to follow Christ and used their gifts to serve God.

Since none of us lived in Bible times to witness the supernatural occurrences for ourselves, we should not be dogmatic about the issue.[1]

---

1. The late Chinese pastor and author Watchman Nee wrote *The Latent Power of the Soul* (Richmond, VA: Christian Fellowship, 1972), in which he theorized that God created the first humans with an innate ability to perform miraculous feats, but when they sinned, these special powers became dormant and buried within their soul. Some people, according to Nee, have learned how to reactivate or release these latent but fallen faculties. When manifested, they

On the Matter of Demonic Manifestations

The earliest Christ followers held that they were uniquely filled with God's Spirit and empowered to perform supernatural acts. They looked suspiciously on "outsiders" who did similar feats and believed they did Satan's bidding. In some cases, Jesus and the apostles confronted the enemies of God and cast demons out of them. In one case, the apostle Paul expelled a demon from a fortune-teller, and she lost her power (Acts 16:16–18).

Based on these scriptural accounts of first-century exorcism, shouldn't we consider the possibility that some modern psychics are demon possessed? Many theologians and members of the clergy think so, especially among those who accept the Bible as an authoritative guide for belief and practice. However, others — even Christians — see things a bit differently. They argue that what the nascent church identified as demon possession was actually schizophrenia (unknown at the time).

According to Kenneth L. Pike (1912–2000), linguist, anthropologist, and first president of the Summer Institute of Linguistics, there are two *equal* ways we can interpret Scripture. The first is known as the "emic" approach, which means we accept the perspective of the people who lived in Bible times.[2] Biblical characters, like all ancients, without access to modern scientific knowledge, thought like everyone else in their day and age. They viewed paranormal wonders through a supernatural lens.[3] When I preach and interpret the text, I take an

---

function as psychic or soulish gifts. However, they differ from spiritual gifts that the Holy Spirit gives only to born-again believers (1 Cor. 12:4–11; 1 Pet. 4:10).

2. Pike used the emic/etic distinction to designate two complementary standpoints for analyzing human language and behavior. See Kenneth L. Pike, *Language in Relation to a Unified Theory of the Structure of Human Behavior*, 2nd rev. ed. (The Hague: Moulton, 1967), and *Talk, Thought, and Thing: The Emic Road toward Conscious Knowledge* (Dallas: Summer Institute of Linguistics, 1993). Also, see Bruce J. Malina and John J. Pilch, *Social Science Commentary on the Book of Acts* (Minneapolis: Fortress, 2008), 101.

3. Ancients also accepted other cultural and sociological beliefs of their day.

emic approach and explain what the biblical text says and what events meant in their original context.

The second method of biblical interpretation is known as the "etic" approach, which means we analyze the culture and events in the Scriptures from the perspective of an outsider, in our case, as moderns. What the people in Bible times viewed as demon possession, we might understand today as a psychiatric condition. This may account for the rarity of modern-day demon possession in Western civilization. Paul Meier, MD, a respected psychiatrist and evangelical Christian, says that every case of "demon possession" he ever treated turned out to be something else.[4]

The Roman Catholic Church still maintains an office of exorcist and trains priests to perform the "Rite of Exorcism." But according to the Vatican's latest guidelines (1999), medical doctors must *first* examine so-called possessed people to make certain they are not suffering from clinical psychosis. This precaution has reduced sanctioned exorcisms to a minuscule number.

On the Matter of Ouija Boards, Pendulums, and Divining Rods

Joseph Jastrow (1863–1944), the Polish-born American psychologist, invented the automagraph, a machine that detected unconscious hand movement and showed that when we concentrate on an object our body gives off nearly imperceptible signals (ideomotor movements) in the direction of the object. This explains how and why the Ouija board indicator works. If, for example, I ask, "Ouija, where was I born?," the

---

For example, the earth was the center of the universe and the sun encircled it. It was not until Copernicus (1473–1543) that we learned that the sun was at the center of our solar system.

4. Dan Korem and Paul Meier, *The Fakers: Exploding the Myths of the Supernatural*, rev. ed. (Grand Rapids: Baker Books, 1980), 162. One can believe in the devil and evil without characterizing most psychic manifestations as being demonic.

planchette will spell out the correct answer. While it may seem like an otherworldly source or mysterious power is moving the planchette, in reality my subconscious mind is directing my hands.[5] Pendulums and divining rods operate on the same principle.

Everybody — to one degree or another — exhibits involuntary gestures that telegraph personal information or attitudes. Perceptive people can spot these *tells* or reflexes and use them for their own advantage. By spotting an opponent's unintentional cue, a card sharp, for example, knows when to raise the ante or fold his hand. In spite of putting on a "poker face," most players cannot hide unconscious tics and reflexes. Therefore, many wear sunglasses or hats with a brim pulled down over their face.

A *tell* can inform an astute salesperson when to stop selling and when to start closing the deal. It also helps parents know when their child is lying or telling the truth. We've all heard the saying, "Some people can be read like a book." This means they cannot hide their emotions, positive or negative. Think of former president George W. Bush, when Andy Card leaned over and told him about the 9/11 attack. Bush's face said it all! These unconscious muscle movements indirectly reveal what a person is thinking or how she or he is responding to a set of circumstances. The best mind readers, clairvoyants, and psychic seers unconsciously depend on their ability to discern almost unnoticeable ideomotor responses when they seek to divine a client's future.

ON THE MATTER OF PSYCHIC FRAUDS

Only relatively *few* psychics have an intuitive ability to pick up cues and signs from their clients; the majority, especially those who tout their psychic prowess on TV or in the grocery store tabloids, are charlatans and fakers. The evidence supports this conclusion. When have

5. If, by chance, I do not know how to spell a word, the Ouija will misspell it as well. Or if I don't know the answer to a question, the Ouija will give an incorrect reply.

you heard of a psychic winning the lottery, or a miracle worker healing the sick in a Covid or cancer ward? If their powers were real, they would all be rich and our hospitals empty. We must beware of those who make extraordinary claims.

Most TV psychics accomplish their so-called feats through trickery. For example, a psychic can make multiple predictions about a national election. To a group in Eugene, Oregon, she predicts candidate A will win. In Bangor, Maine, the following week, she predicts candidate B. A month later in Omaha, Nebraska, she predicts candidate C. The local newspaper in each town runs the story. Whichever candidate triumphs, the psychic produces the newspaper clipping as evidence she has special powers.

Years ago, I read about a California psychic who accurately identified who would kill J. R. Ewing, the lead character on the popular 1980s TV show *Dallas*. ABC interviewed him live from its New York studio an hour before the airing. Everyone was astonished when his prediction proved true! Come to find out he had already watched the show when it had aired earlier on the West Coast.

ON THE MATTER OF HEALING

Because Western medicine is scientifically advanced above all other systems, many physicians treat alternative medicine as either primitive or quackery. Only of late has the medical establishment taken seriously the connection between mind and body and the part the subconscious plays in the healing process. In 1998, the National Institutes of Health, the federal government's lead agency for scientific research, established the National Center for Complementary and Integrative Health to investigate rigorously alternative approaches to health.

Our Amazing Immune System and Subconscious Mind

Our immune system is the body's internal doctor that combats sickness, injury, and disease. If we take proper care of ourselves — eating a balanced diet, exercising, and living stress-free — our immune system can handle most of our physical needs.[6] But when we abuse our bodies, the immune system has to work overtime.

In addition to our immune system, our subconscious mind (i.e., the brain operating at the alpha, theta, and delta speeds) contains a storehouse of knowledge and wisdom that we can tap and gain insight into healing. Solutions often come while we meditate or sleep (via dreams, strong impressions, metaphors, imagery, flashes of inspiration, or an inner voice). Just like a car's computer, our brain can analyze the problem and suggest a course of action. According to Judith Orloff, MD, assistant professor of psychiatry at UCLA, we all possess an "intuitive healing code" (written in an encrypted or metaphorical language) that we can access. But we must learn to decipher it.[7]

For those of us unable to access our subconscious mind, we can seek help from physicians, psychiatrists, psychologists, and other specialists trained in psychoneurological sciences. Some function at an intuitive level and rely on their vast knowledge and their own subconscious minds to pick up cues, spot symptoms, make accurate diagnoses, and offer creative solutions. Their abilities appear to border on the paranormal.

For example, in some Inuit cultures, a sick person is brought to the shaman, who dances, sings, burns incense, chants repetitively, and performs other rituals until the sufferer slips into a trance, an indication that "the spirits" are at work. The shaman then offers suggestions for healing and recovery. When the patient returns to consciousness, she

---

6. Repressing our emotions can contribute to ill health and disease, while catharsis can offer benefits. When we cry and laugh, we release our emotions. In the book of Proverbs we read, "A cheerful heart is a good medicine, / but a downcast spirit dries up the bones" (Prov. 17:22). We've all heard "Laughter is the best medicine." It is more than an old wives' tale. According to the Harvard Medical School and Mayo Clinic, laughter relaxes the body, reduces stress, boosts the immune system, relieves pain, increases blood flow, and releases endorphins, a feel-good hormone that produces euphoric feelings.

7. Judith Orloff, *Intuitive Healing* (New York: Random House, 2000), 1–43.

feels better and her health improves significantly. While the Inuits may erroneously attribute healing to the spirits, their shaman is the wise person who knows the secret to restoration, and the rituals trigger the subconscious mind to work its magic.

Limitations of Our Immune System and Subconscious Mind

While it is important to understand the power of the immune system and the subconscious mind, some physical problems can be remedied only with the help of direct medical intervention. My granddaughter recently tripped and fell down the stairway, breaking her ankle in several places. The repair required the knowledge of a skilled surgeon, a three-hour operation, setting the broken bones with eight long screws, and two steel plates. Even after four months, her ankle still swells and she feels pain. The recovery process will be prolonged.

A friend of mine — a preacher and man of faith — inadvertently poked his grandson's eye with a sharp dart. There was only one way to save his sight — emergency surgery!

Combat soldiers face untold dangers, including snipers' bullets, shrapnel, and land mines. Unfortunately, for some, the dangers become realities. We have all seen soldiers with a patch over an eye, missing limbs, or reconstructed faces.

I recently had cataract surgery. Without it, my vision would continue to deteriorate. We all find ourselves in need of medical attention at times, whether for a toothache, hypertension, or a heart transplant. Once a medical procedure is performed, the immune system seeks to complete the healing process.

ON THE MATTER OF BREATHING

Breath is the animating force of life. Without it we cannot live. The Hebrew Scriptures provide an account of human creation. It asserts that the first human (Adam) was created out of the dust of the ground. His body lay lifeless and needed to be animated or energized. According to this tradition, God "breathed into his nostrils the *breath* of life" (Gen. 2:7). As a result, Adam became a bipartite being, composed of earthly (human) and heavenly (divine) components.

Like Adam, we all take a first breath (*inspiration*) at birth, and one day we will take our last (*expiration*).[8] Between these two points, breathing (*respiration*) is our constant companion. Unfortunately, most of us do not breathe properly. Our brains — operating at beta speed — become overtaxed, and our breathing becomes shallow. Consequently, we often become fatigued and find ourselves yawning. Our brainwaves automatically slow down, giving our critical minds and our five senses a much-needed rest as our breathing becomes more relaxed.

Rhythmic Breathing

Many ancient civilizations taught the art of slow, rhythmic breathing, which they believed was the secret to wholeness. Yogic breathing techniques found in regions of the Himalayan Mountains and the Indus Valley date back five millennia. Yoga masters equate *prana* (Sanskrit word for breath) with the "life-force" or "vital energy" that flows through the body.[9] The Chinese version is *ch'i* or *Qi*.[10] The Japanese, *ki*.[11] The Hebrew, *ru'ach*. The Greek, *pneuma*.

---

8. As the inspired poet writes, "For everything there is a season, and a time for every matter under heaven: a time to be born, and a time to die" (Eccles. 3:1–2). He goes on to say, the body returns to the earth and our breath (*ru'ach*) returns to God, who gave it (12:7). James echoed this sentiment in the New Testament: "The body *apart from the spirit* is dead" (James 2:26 ESV). As Jesus hung on a cross, he cried out with a loud voice, "'Father, into your hands I commend *my spirit.*' Having said this, *he breathed his last*" (Luke 23:46).

9. James Nestor, *Breath: The New Science of a Lost Art* (New York: Penguin, 2020), 195–96.

10. Chinese rely on Qi Gong, meaning "breath work" (slow deep diaphragmatic breathing), to enhance or restore bodily energy.

11. Nestor, *Breath*, 188.

Native American tribes identify breath or vital energy variously as *orenda* (Iroquois and Huron tribes), *orenna* (Cayuga, and Oneida, Mohawk), *mahopa* (Sioux), *manitowi* (Algonquin), and *pokunt* (Shoshoni). Practitioners among Native Americans believe that individuals can control or manipulate this energy through prayer, rituals, music, and dance.

Researchers at Stanford, Harvard, Menninger and Mayo clinics, and the National Institutes of Health are seriously investigating the mind-body connection and the relationship of proper breathing to our overall health. "Breathing is a power switch to a vast network called the autonomic nervous system"[12] that consists of two sections. (1) The parasympathetic — a network of nerves located in the lower lungs — regulates bodily functions, such as heart rate, emotions, tear ducts, saliva glands, digestion, relaxation and restoration, and sexual stimulation, among others. (2) The sympathetic — nerves located in the top region of the lungs — sends messages to the body to prepare for fight or flight and is activated in stressful and dangerous situations as our breathing becomes fast and shallow. Once the crisis passes, we feel sapped of energy and emotionally drained.[13]

Rhythmic Breathing and Nitric Oxide

Not all breathing is the same. The difference between nose and mouth breathing, for example, is significant. Scientific testing confirms that nasal breathing boosts the production of nitric oxide (NO) by 18 percent over mouth breathing. Nitric oxide is a powerful molecule that widens our capillaries, relaxes our smooth muscles, and delivers oxygen to the cells.[14] When we let go of our problems and worries, breathe deeply through our nose and relax, an amazing thing happens. NO is released in a series of small puffs of gas into the bloodstream. This,

12. Nestor, *Breath*, 144.
13. Nestor, *Breath*, 144–45.
14. Nestor, *Breath*, 50, 223.

in turn, triggers the production of endorphins and dopamine, that is, neurotransmitters that enhance feelings of well-being and reduce pain.[15] The deeper we breathe, the better we feel.

Hebert Benson, MD, called nitric oxide the body's "internal wind," or the biological equivalent of the Spirit that energizes us and enables us to perform effortlessly at our peak.[16] This may partially explain the phenomenon described as "being in the zone." Scientists are now studying to see if NO is also a contributing factor when an athlete gets a *second wind* — a burst of energy that enables a performer to run more swiftly than when he or she started.

Rhythmic Breathing and Transcendence

Deep nasal breathing and the concomitant release of NO may also serve as the gateway to transcendental experiences and eureka moments.

Many Eastern yoga teachers emphasize the importance of breathing through the *nostrils*. Chinese Taoists of the eighth century BCE called the nose the door to heaven. Modern-day meditators often claim that as they relax by breathing through the nose, they slip into an altered state of consciousness and sense God's presence. Interestingly, the Hebrew Scriptures note that God "breathed into [Adam's] *nostrils* the breath of life" (Gen. 2:7). In the book of Job, arguably the oldest book in the Bible, Job characterizes God's spirit as being "*in my nostrils*" (Job 27:3 ESV).

Scientists have now hypothesized that we all possess a biological capacity for the divine. When we pray, meditate, and worship, certain physiological or chemical changes take place in our brains that

15. Herbert Benson, MD, and William Proctor, *The Break-Out Principle* (New York: Scribner, 2003), 27, 48. Joan Borysenko, cofounder of the Mind/Body Clinic at Deaconess Hospital (Boston) and instructor in medicine at Harvard Medical School, advocates using the breath to let go of pain. Joan Borysenko, *Minding the Body, Mending the Mind* (Reading, MA: Addison-Wesley, 1987), 86.

16. Benson and Proctor, *The Break-Out Principle*, 65.

can be measured with modern scientific tools such as PET scan and fMRI. If correct, transcendence can be experienced by us all, regardless of our particular religion, for example, Hindu, Buddhist, Animist, or Christian.[17]

ON THE MATTER OF FAITH

Here we will deal with faith as it interacts with two areas: our well-being and our performance.

Faith and Our Well-Being

Faith triggers biochemical responses in our body and also plays a role in our physical well-being. Our bodies respond both to positive and negative thoughts.[18] The Gospels tell of a woman with an issue of blood who had been sick for twelve years. After hearing about Jesus's healing ministry, she said to herself, "If I can only touch the hem of his garment, I will be made well." Obviously, Jesus's robe had no innate healing power, but she was healed instantaneously. How so? As Jesus explained to her: "Daughter, your *faith* has made you well" (Luke 8:48).

On another occasion, Jesus encountered a man who had been blind from birth. Wanting to help, Jesus spat on the ground and mixed his saliva with the dirt, turning it into mud. He then applied it to the man's eyes and instructed, "Go, wash in the pool of Siloam." The man did as told and received his sight (John 9:6–7). Since mud is devoid of

17. This thesis is based on the premise that we all possess the *divine* breath and thus have a capacity to experience God. We must be careful, however, not to equate a transcendental experience with salvation, which is another issue altogether.

18. "Rumination" is the psychological term for constant mental distress associated with worry and anxiety and is considered a risk factor for clinical depression.

medicinal properties, how was the man healed? The only plausible answer is faith.

After years of research, Herb Benson, MD, concluded, "The data is undeniable. Faith is indeed central to life and health."[19] It can jump-start our sluggish immune system. The object of faith can be a family doctor, a skilled surgeon, an acupuncturist, or homeopath, a medication, a sugar pill, a witch's brew, a healing prayer, or even a shamanistic or religious ritual.

Every year multitudes of people — many with incurable diseases — make pilgrimages to sacred shrines and grottoes. One of the most famous is the Fountain of Lourdes in southwestern France, where in 1858 a young girl named Bernadette testified that the Virgin Mary appeared and ordered her to dig a hole in the ground and drink of the water that would gush forth. As the story spread, curious townspeople visited the site and imbibed from the newly formed spring. Some reported being healed of various illnesses. Today, over five million pilgrims a year make the trek to drink the so-called *curative* waters. Tests have proven that the water is nothing more than H2O. Yet, according to the Roman Catholic Church, numerous documented healings occur annually.[20]

Faith is powerful, but it's also mysterious. We cannot simply turn it on and off like a faucet, as some claim. Therefore, we must be careful not to mistake presumption for faith.

Early on in my career, I attended a charismatic meeting where the speaker urged his listeners who needed a healing to step out in faith and claim it. I did as instructed and took off my eyeglasses that I wore

19. Herbert Benson with Marg Stark, *Timeless Healing: The Power and Biology of Belief* (New York: Scribner's Sons, 1990), 191.

20. About twice a year, my mother persuaded me to drive her to a small grotto of Mother Seton located in Emmitsburg, Maryland. Most days only a few visited the site. According to Roman Catholic tradition, Seton prayed successfully in 1952 for Ann O'Neil, a four-year-old with leukemia. After verifying the "miracle," the church beatified Seton and later named her a saint (1975). Now multitudes flock there.

for nearsightedness. The next day, having left my glasses at home, I drove across the country to attend a professional conference. The trip was uneventful until dusk, when I approached the outskirts of Gary, Indiana. Factory smoke hovered over the city and blocked out the remaining sunlight. My vision diminished even more when night fell. The lines on the highway looked blurred, and I couldn't read the exit signs. I was in trouble, and my glasses were sitting on my dresser seven hundred miles away. It was a hard-learned lesson. I had acted in presumption, not faith.

Unfortunately, we do not understand how or why faith is activated in some people and not others. It is beyond our ability to control. Yet, when it is triggered in the brain by an unexpected word, event, sight, thought, or serendipitous encounter, doubts cease and amazing things happen. Harold Koenig, MD, associate professor of psychiatry and behavioral sciences and professor of medicine at Duke University Medical Center, devotes an entire book to an examination of faith, which he calls the "last great frontier" of medicine.[21]

Faith and Our Performance

Faith is not limited to physical healing. It can also produce confidence to achieve goals and overcome barriers. A person may trust and act on the advice of a tarot card reader, fortune-teller, religious leader, or other authoritative voice. He or she may believe in the efficacy of a secret chant, a formula, magic words (e.g., "abracadabra"), guidance from a Ouija board, or the counsel of a trance medium. Once the imagination is triggered and the subconscious mind accepts the faith proposition, remarkable things happen!

Jesus instructs his followers: "Have faith in God. Truly I tell you, if you say to this *mountain,* 'Be taken up and thrown into the sea,' and if you do not doubt in your heart, but believe that what you say will

---

21. Harold G. Koenig, *The Healing Power of Faith: Science Explores Medicine's Last Great Frontier* (New York: Simon & Schuster, 2001).

come to pass, it will be done for you. So I tell you, *whatever* you ask for in prayer, believe that you have received it, and it will be yours" (Mark 11:23–24).

Metaphorically speaking, "mountain" refers to the insurmountable, whether obstacles or goals. The term "whatever" is all-encompassing. In essence, Jesus says the power of faith is without limits.

Jesus concludes with a command: "Believe that you have received it [that it is ours already in the present], and it will be yours [in the future; no ifs, ands, or buts about it]." These words constitute a hard saying. In our *mind's eye* we must see the desired outcome as ours even before it arrives. Hence, faith and imagination go hand in hand.[22] The subconscious mind grabs hold of the promise and accepts it as reality! Without imagination, faith is deficient.

In Matthew's version of the above account, Jesus says, "If you have faith the size of a mustard seed, you will say to this mountain, 'Move from here to there,' and it will move, and nothing will be impossible for you" (Matt. 17:20). Note that the issue is not the quantity of our faith but the quality of the faith. The smallest amount of authentic faith can produce the largest results. Impossibilities become reality.

To give a real-life example of the power of faith, we need look no further than to the world of track and field. For years, experts said it was physically impossible to run the distance of a mile in less than four minutes. The human body was not equipped for the task. But on

---

22. The writer of Hebrews puts it this way: "Faith is the substance of things hoped for, the evidence of things not seen" (Heb. 11:1 KJV). Notice, faith is (1) substance and (2) evidence "of the thing hoped for" but "not [yet] seen." It grasps as reality what our five natural senses fail to comprehend. It is a sixth sense. Unfortunately, in an age of skepticism, many of us want empirical evidence *before* we believe. We live by the adage, "Seeing is believing." Faith is the opposite. It says, "Believing is seeing."

The only thing that limited Jesus's power was the people's lack of faith. His hometown crowd did not view him as a miracle worker: "And he could do no deed of power there, except that he laid his hands on a few sick people and cured them. And he was amazed at their unbelief" (Mark 6:5–6).

May 6, 1954, British speedster Roger Bannister ran a mile in 3:59.4 minutes. Within two months the record was broken twice more! Since Bannister's record, the four-minute mile has been broken over sixteen hundred times. What changed? The distance was the same. The human body was the same. The only thing that differed was *a belief* that running that fast was now possible. Other runners soon *imagined* themselves breaking the mark. Once they realized it could be done, faith enabled them to accomplish the feat.

ON THE MATTER OF MIRACLES

We classify rare events that defy all known laws of nature as miracles. We believe in miracles *because* we believe in a deity who sovereignly and occasionally (at the behest of his followers) intervenes in human affairs. Since miracles are *supernatural* and *unique*, they cannot be verified by *natural* means or *replicated* in a lab. Neither medicine nor the subconscious mind offers an explanation. They are unfathomable mysteries.[23]

A PERSONAL WORD

When it comes to paranormal phenomena, I have only touched the tip of the iceberg. I hope this book has stimulated your curiosity enough for you to keep up with the exciting field of mind-body research. I highly recommend for further reading the books listed in the bibliography, especially those dealing with neurotheology, a new category of neuroscience that seeks to understand the integration of religion and the brain. As an added aid to help you master the unusual vocabulary associated with paranormal studies, I have included a glossary of terms with concise definitions of key words used throughout the book.

23. For example, the Christian Scriptures recount how God used Jesus to restore life to a dead man whose body lay rotting in a tomb for four days and had begun to smell (John 11:1–44). We simply read such an account with awe and wonder.

You have all the internal resources — physical, spiritual, and psychological — needed to live a wonderful and fulfilled life. Don't waste your time on frivolous activities, worry, negative thoughts, and destructive behaviors. Life is too short. One day it will be over. As the inspired poet writes, "For everything there is a season, and a time for every matter under heaven: a time to be born, / and a time to die" (Eccles. 3:1–2). He goes on to say, the body returns to the earth and our breath (*ru'ach*) returns to God, who gave it (12:7). James echoed this sentiment in the New Testament: "The body apart from the spirit is dead" (James 2:26 ESV). Even Jesus announced from the cross, "Father, into your hands I commend my spirit." He then "breathed his last" (Luke 23:46).

So, between now and then, relax, breathe deeply, laugh a lot, enjoy life, allow your imagination to run wild, and let your dreams work their magic.

Acknowledgments

Writing for publication is a multifaceted process and takes a team effort. While an author writes a book, others carry it to completion.

My wife, Lynn, read and reread every word of my manuscript. She spotted errors and informed me when I failed to communicate clearly. Her eagle eye and attention to detail complemented my ability to tell the big story.

Daniel and Andrew Streett, biblical scholars and authors in their own right, also read the manuscript and offered well-reasoned theological advice.

When I finished writing *Exploring the Paranormal* and casually mentioned it in a social media post, James Ernest, editor in chief of Eerdmans, asked if he could read it. A few days later he texted to say my book was "a real page turner" and recommended that I submit it to Eerdmans. Thank you, James, for your support and advocacy.

James McGrath, scholar, bibliophile, and Renaissance man, wrote a most interesting foreword, in which he not only captured the spirit of my memoir but explained why it is an important contribution to the field of spirituality. Make sure to read how the book personally impacted him. His insights have added immeasurably to the value of this book.

Laurel Draper, the consummate project editor, handled the day-to-day process of getting my manuscript ready for publication. What a joy to work with such a kind and competent professional. I always felt my book was in good hands.

Tom Raabe, a clear-thinking wordsmith and copyeditor, made sure my vocabulary choices and sentence structures conveyed exactly what I intended. Whenever he recommended changes, they improved the quality of my writing. Thanks, Tom.

Shane White and his team have worked hard to promote *Exploring the Paranormal*. Shane, who creatively thinks outside the box, is my kind of person. If this book is a retail success, it will be largely due to his efforts.

Jonathan Merritt, Joel Green, Gordon Melton, Harold Koenig, and Lisa Miller, all well-known authors and experts in their respective fields, wrote strong endorsements. Thank you for your kind words of support.

Finally, I wish to thank all who joined my Facebook book launch group, preordered the book, and wrote reviews to encourage others to read it.

GLOSSARY

Abracadabra. An ancient incantation inscribed in triangle form on amulets and worn to ward off evil spirits and heal diseases. Serenus Sammonicus, physician to the Roman emperor Caracalla from AD 211 to 212, was the first to prescribe the method. In modern times, stage magicians often use the word when performing a trick.

A B R A C A D A B R A

A B R A C A D A B R

A B R A C A D A B

A B R A C A D A

A B R A C A D

A B R A C A

A B R A C

A B R A

A B R

A B

A

Affirmations. Positive declarations spoken aloud in the present tense in order to produce future results.

Akashic records. The totality of the world's knowledge that is theoretically stored on the ethereal plane. Some psychics believe they can access this information while in a trance state.

Alchemy. The purported secret art of transforming base metals into precious metals, which has been lost over time.

Alpha brainwaves. Electrical currents that travel in the brain during the day when a person is daydreaming or meditating.

Altered state of consciousness (ASC). The condition that results when a person transitions out of a mental state of alertness (beta) into an alpha, theta, or delta state. Altered states usually occur spontaneously but can also be achieved by hypnosis, psychedelic drugs, or meditation.

Amulets. Charms or objects believed to have magical powers that protect wearers from evil spirits and bad luck.

Animal magnetism. A magnetic force that purportedly flows through the human body and causes sickness when it is blocked or out of balance. Franz Mesmer, the Viennese physician, believed he could manipulate this force and bring about healing. His theory was later disproved.

Apports. Physical objects or trinkets supposedly sent from the spirit world that materialize during a séance.

Archetypes. The unconscious metaphoric thought patterns that have evolved over time and have become part of our collective DNA as humans. These universal patterns or themes find expression in our literature, art, and mythical tales.

Ascended master. A sage or advanced soul who has reached a high level of spiritual maturity in the ethereal world and now communicates wisdom to those on the earth plane.

Association for Research and Enlightenment (ARE). A nonprofit organization located in Virgina Beach, VA, that conducts research into the life and work of Edgar Cayce.

Astral projection. The separation of the soul from the body, enabling it to travel with little or no hindrance to various spiritual realms of the universe.

Astrology. A pseudoscience that teaches that the movement of the planets governs human affairs.

Aura. An invisible force or iridescence that surrounds the human body and is discernible only by those with psychic powers. Auras emanate various hues that indicate a person's physical state of well-being.

Automatic writing. Messages received from the spirit world or the subconscious mind and transcribed by the receiver.

Autonomic nervous system. A network of nerves that regulates the internal organs that are not subject to human volition.

Autosuggestion. A repeated affirmation that generates a favorable outcome in the future.

Beta brainwaves. Electrical currents that travel in the brain when a person is wide awake and interacts with the world.

Biorhythms. Physical, emotional, and mental cycles that theoretically overlap and occasionally converge, producing opportunities for optimal decision making.

Blue Book. A listing of people (along with information about them) who regularly visit psychic advisors. Subscribing psychics receive and share the data with each other in order to give their clients consistent readings.

Breath work. The practice of rhythmic breathing from the diaphragm with the intended goal of reaching an altered state of consciousness.

Centering prayer. A combination of rhythmic breathing and repeating a sacred word or mantra in order to experience God's presence.

Chakras. Seven centers along the spinal column from its base to the top of the head through which energy flows. Similar to acupuncture's meridian points and Mesmer's heavenly tides.

Channeler. A trance medium who serves as a conduit between the spirit and physical worlds, and conveys messages from one sphere to the other.

Circadian rhythm. The body's twenty-four-hour internal clock that regulates our brainwaves and energy levels. The circadian rhythm is divided into ultradian segments lasting 90–120 minutes.

Clairvoyance. The ability to see things others do not. A person possessing this power is called a clairvoyant or seer.

Cold reading. A method psychics use to glean information on a new client based on ideomotor movements, dress, accents, jewelry, body language, and verbal responses. The information is later fed back to the client in the form of psychic insight.

Conjurer. An amateur or professional magician who performs tricks and illusions for entertainment purposes.

Cryptomnesia. The phenomenon whereby memories are recalled but are regarded as new or original by the person recalling them. Often occurs in past life regression sessions under the guidance of a hypnotist.

Crystal ball. A translucent orb into which psychics gaze to divine the future for sitters.

Crystals. Special energized stones used to heal or produce spiritual well-being.

Cues. Nearly invisible tells or involuntary movements that skilled observers can detect and interpret, revealing information about their subject.

Déjà vu. A phenomenon that occurs when a person perceives that he or she is undergoing an experience he or she has had before.

Demon possession. The bodily indwelling of an evil spirit and its take-over of the human personality.

Delta brainwaves. The slowest electrical currents that operate in the brain when a person is in deep sleep.

Dissociation. A disconnection between a person's five senses and the world around the person. According to many psychological studies, psychic mediums experience temporary dissociation when they enter a trance, often resulting in loss of memory, self-identity, and consciousness of their surroundings.

Divination. The act of predicting the future through various occult means, such as palmistry, scrying, reading tea leaves, casting astrological charts, and consulting the *I Ching*, Ouija board, and pendulum.

Dowsing. An unreliable means of discovering underground resources such as water, oil, or precious ores through the use of a Y-shaped branch or metal rod that guides and points down to a location.

Drawing out fire. Supposedly removing pain from burn victims by waving hands above the burns and repeating secret words.

Ectoplasm. A visible substance purported to emanate from a trance medium's orifice during a séance that wraps itself around the ethereal body of a spirit so its form can be seen.

Electroencephalogram (EEG). A test to measure the electrical currents in the brain. When brainwave activity ceases, an individual is declared brain-dead.

Extrasensory perception (ESP). The capacity to receive information or perform physical tasks without reliance on external sources. The term, coined by J. B. Rhine, encompasses all kinds of paranormal abilities ranging from telepathy (transference of thoughts from one person to another) to psychokinesis (moving physical objects with the mind alone).

Faith. Belief or trust in a person, object, or thing — real or imagined — that gives us confidence of a desired outcome. Faith is essential in activating the placebo effect.

Faith healing. Physical cures that are triggered by a person's trust or faith in God, a healer, a placebo, or some other nonmedical modality.

Fakir. A Hindu holy man from India who has mastered self-discipline and yogic exercises and is known for his paranormal abilities.

Fortune-telling. The supposed ability to predict the future through occult means such as astrology and reading tarot cards.

Full Gospel Business Men's Fellowship International (FGBMFI). Nonprofit evangelistic organization founded by Demos and Rose Shakarian to reach business people with the gospel of Christ and promote charismatic gifts.

Functional magnetic resonance imagery (fMRI). A test that identifies certain kinds of brain activity based on increased blood flow to various areas of the cerebral cortex. When one prays, for example, additional blood gushes into the periventricular gray matter of the hypothalamus.

Glossolalia. The phenomenon of speaking in an unknown and unlearned language, earthly or heavenly, by means of the Holy Spirit.

Graphology. The art of determining an individual's personality, moral character, quirks, and emotional stability through handwriting analysis.

Guru. A teacher or spiritual master who has students or followers that believe that their leader possesses advanced wisdom.

Hallucination. False sensory experience that seems real but is nonexistent according to objective data.

Homeopathy. A healing method of prescribing infinitesimal amounts of substances composed of elements similar to the disease itself. It is based on the theory that "like cures like."

Hot reading. The psychic practice of researching clients before giving them a reading and then passing off the information as coming from a supernatural source.

Hyperacusis. An ability to hear sounds and voices from great distances, even when separated by soundproof barriers.

Hypnagogic. Relating to the transitory period when one begins to enter sleep or comes out of sleep, when one is groggy.

Hypnosis. An altered state of consciousness or trance-like state that involves focused attention to suggestions and limited awareness of surroundings as the brain activity slows to alpha speed. Hypnosis can be self-induced or induced by a hypnotist.

Hypnosis Motivation Institute (HMI). The first college of hypnotherapy in America to be nationally accredited. Founded by John Kappas.

I Ching. An ancient Chinese divination manual that predicts the future based on the principle of yin/yang and is used to provide guidance for daily living and decision making.

Ideomotor movement. An almost imperceptible bodily action generated by the subconscious mind that often reveals what a person is thinking. Ideomotor reactions are believed to be the modus operandi behind the movement of the pendulum, divining rod, and planchette across the Ouija board.

Incantation. A secret word, formula, or saying that invokes the aid of spirits or is used to place a hex on someone.

Incubus. A male spirit, often a demon, that visits a sleeping female at night for the purpose of having sex.

Inner healing. A psycho-spiritual therapeutic cure grounded in a belief that many illnesses are the result of past hurts and unresolved conflicts. The technique involves regressing the ailing person back to the source of the problem through guided imagery and inviting Jesus to come into the scene, who is able to resolve the past issues, resulting in healing.

Intuition. A subconscious hunch or sense of knowing something without empirical input.

Karma. The law of cause and effect. Often associated with reincarnation. The choices we make in this lifetime will determine our lot in the next incarnation.

Kirlian photography. A photographic technique developed in the 1960s that purportedly captured the images of the aura or energy field that surrounds the human body. Further tests and experimentation proved the process to be flawed and the results discredited.

Kundalini. Serpent power or sexual energy that lies coiled and dormant at the base of the spine, which rises after prolonged yogic exercises and passes through the seven chakras uniting the person with God.

Laying on of hands. A technique used by Christians and occult practitioners to facilitate physical healing, which is attributed to the transference of the Holy Spirit or energy from the body of the healer to the seeker.

Levitation. The act of floating off the ground without the aid of physical means. An unproven paranormal act of defying the law of gravity.

Mantra. A word that is repeated silently on the in-breath and out-breath during mediation. The purpose is to keep focused and limit outside distractions.

Materialization. The act of persons or objects from the spirit world manifesting physically during a séance. Serves as evidence that communication with the dead is real. A prominent feature during the heyday of physical mediumship.

Mentalism. A branch of professional magic, also known as mental magic, that centers on psychic-style magic tricks, for example, mind reading, precognition, and telekinesis.

Meridians. In acupuncture, twelve invisible channels in the body through which energy passes.

Mesmerism. An early form of hypnosis popularized by Franz Mesmer and based on the erroneous theory that heavenly tides or magnetic forces permeate the body, which can be manipulated to bring about healing.

Mind. The capacity in a person that feels, thinks, and reasons. The mind and brain are intricately connected with thinking as one function of the brain. Apart from the brain, the mind does not exist.

Miracle. A supernatural occurrence that defies all known laws of nature.

Muscle reading. A technique used by mentalists to determine a person's thoughts or find hidden objects. Also known as "contact mind reading."

Necromancy. Communication with the dead by means of divination.

Numerology. The application of numbers, a combination of numbers, or mathematical calculations to a person's name or birth date to determine the person's future.

Nitric oxide (NO). A colorless gas molecule that enhances the immune system, circulatory system, and athletic performance. Increases in NO levels in the bloodstream are associated with a "runner's high" and getting a "second wind."

Occam's razor. A philosophical rule asserting that the simplest solution is usually the best solution. Complicated and convoluted answers and conspiracy theories usually yield little or no results.

Occult. Relating to secret or hidden knowledge that can be accessed only through paranormal means. From the Latin, meaning hidden or obscure.

Omen. A sign that something significant has or is about to take place. Often associated with flight of birds, known as augury.

Oracle of Delphi. An ancient Greek seeress called Pythia who prophesied and spoke on behalf of Apollo as she sat on a tripod in the temple at Delphi.

Ouija board. A rectangular board with two rows of letters in the center and numbers 1–9 at the bottom. An accompanying heart-shaped pointer, called a planchette, mysteriously moves over the board to spell out words, give dates, and offer advice when two people place their fingertips on it.

Palm reader. A person who claims the ability to predict the future by reading and analyzing the lines on other people's palms. Also known as chiromancy.

Panentheism. A worldview that teaches all that exists is part of God but God is more than the sum total of all things.

Pantheism. A worldview that teaches that all is God. It is based on the premise that there is only one level of reality.

Paramnesia. A condition or phenomenon in which memories become distorted over time or have been implanted into the mind by a hypnotist, psychotherapist, or counselor.

Paranormal. Any action or phenomenon that lies beyond reasonable explanation and does not comply with the laws of nature.

Parapsychology. The scientific study of ESP to determine its validity.

Pendulum. A string or chain with a weighted object at the end. When loosely held, the pendulum begins to sway back and forth or rotate. The movement allows a person to discern truth from error or predict the future. Based on the ideomotor principle.

Phrenology. The pseudoscientific practice of examining the bumps on a person's head to determine the person's personality or future.

Placebo effect. The body's positive response to belief that a treatment or medication will work even if scientifically or medically unproven. One's faith can trigger the placebo effect.

Poltergeist. A loud and mischievous ghost or specter that often haunts a house, frightening the inhabitants.

Precognition. The ability to see into the future or prophesy. Also known as prognostication.

Prestidigitation. The art of performing magic tricks through the use of sleight of hand.

Psi. A Greek letter that is used as an abbreviation for ESP.

Psychokinesis. The ability to move objects with the mind alone.

Psychometry. The purported ability to gain information about a person by touching something the person owns.

Psychosomatic healing. A physical healing of a functional illness that is triggered by the power of belief.

Reflexology. The art of analyzing illness by examining the sole of a person's foot. Treatment involves massaging pressure points on the foot that are connected to various body parts.

Reincarnation. A belief that the soul leaves the body at death and later inhabits another body. With each incarnation, based on the law of karma, the soul moves toward its ultimate goal — absorption into the impersonal Universal Soul (God).

Relaxation response. The positive outcome of deep breathing exercises discovered by Herbert Benson, MD, which enables a person to remain calm in a crisis. The opposite of fight or flight.

Remote viewing. Seeing things or events from a far distance that are not accessible by sight.

Rituals. Repeated ceremonial practices that are prescribed by culture and religion and deemed important for community cohesion.

Scrying. Peering into a crystal ball in an attempt to discern the future.

Séance. A gathering for the purpose of communicating with the departed spirits of the dead through the channel of a trance medium. Also known as "a sitting."

Shaman. A tribal witch doctor, sorcerer, or person of power who can see the future, heal sickness, or invoke the aid of spirits.

Society of American Magicians. A nonprofit organization whose membership is composed of professional and amateur magicians who protect the ways and means of magic and help each other to improve their magical skills.

Somnambulism. The deepest state of hypnotic trance that allows a person to receive and act upon suggestions. When awakened the subject cannot remember what happened.

Sorcerer. An individual who performs feats of magic through use of conjuring, invoking spirits, or mixing of potions.

Spirit guide. A trusted spirit who speaks on behalf of others in the spirit world to the living through the voice of a trance medium.

Spiritual Frontiers Fellowship. An international organization founded in 1956 to promote a belief in the immortality of the soul and to reintroduce the gifts of the Spirit into mainline churches.

Spiritualism. The practice of communicating with the dead (when spelled with a lowercase *s*), or, when spelled with a capital *S*, the religion that grew out of the spiritualist revival in the late 1800s.

Spiritualist camps. Self-contained communities with resident psychics where seekers can receive spiritual guidance, contact dead relatives, and learn to develop their own psychic powers.

Subconscious mind. The thought process when brainwaves move at the alpha, theta, and delta speeds and function with limited or no conscious awareness of the surrounding physical world.

Succubus. A female spirit that visits men in their dreams at night in order to engage in sex.

Talisman. A charm or amulet carried or worn to protect a person from evil and mishap.

Tarot. Any one of a deck of seventy-eight colorful cards decorated on their faces with a variety of esoteric images and symbols and used to predict the future.

Telekinesis. The ability to move objects by means of the mind alone.

Telepathy. The ability to read a person's mind or transfer a thought from one person to another without physical communication or cues.

Teleportation. The paranormal ability to travel from one location to another without means of physical aid.

Tetragrammaton. The unspeakable name of God (YHWH), so sacred that Orthodox Jews use "Adoni" as a substitute when referring to deity.

Theta brainwaves. Electrical currents that travel in the brain as we fall asleep at night or emerge from sleep in the morning.

Trance medium. A person who has the ability to enter an altered state and become a channel of communication between the living and the dead.

Trigger. The inexplicable activation of faith that results in positive outcomes — physical, spiritual, or psychological — otherwise unachievable.

UFO. An unidentified flying object of unknown origin, yet seen by reliable witnesses. Theories about the nature of UFOs range from extraterrestrials to demon manifestations to secret or experimental governmental aircraft.

Yoga. A Hindu discipline that originally combined a variety of physical and mental exercises with a goal of experiencing oneness with God. In the modern West, many people engage in yogic exercises for health purposes only.

Zener cards. A set of five cards, each bearing a different symbol on its face (a circle, a cross, three wavy lines, a square, and a five-pointed star). Zener cards are used to test psychic ability by having a subject guess the symbol on each card to determine whether she or he can score above the level of chance after multiple rounds.

Zodiac. The spherical path the earth travels around the sun, which is divided into twelve 30-degree sectors. Each sector is represented by a sign of the zodiac (Aries, the ram; Taurus, the bull; Gemini, the twins; etc.) and corresponds to thirty-day cycles on the calendar.

BIBLIOGRAPHY

Annemann, Theodore. *Practical Mental Magic*. Brooklyn, NY: D. Robbins, 1944.

Beauregard, Mario, and Denyse O'Leary. *The Spiritual Brain: A Neuroscientist's Case for the Existence of the Soul*. New York: HarperOne, 2007.

Bennett, Dennis. *Nine O'Clock in the Morning*. Plainfield, NJ: Logos, 1970.

Benson, Herbert, with Marg Stark. *Timeless Healing: The Power and Biology of Belief*. New York: Scribner's Sons, 1990.

Benson, Herbert, with Miriam Z. Klipper. *The Relaxation Response*. New York: Morrow, 1975.

Benson, Herbert, with William Proctor. *Beyond the Relaxation Response*. New York: Times Books, 1984.

———. *The Break-Out Principle*. New York: Scribner, 2003.

———. *Relaxation Revolution: Enhancing Your Personal Health through the Science and Genetics of Mind Body Healing*. New York: Scribner's Sons, 2010.

Bernstein, Morey. *The Search for Bridey Murphy*. Garden City, NY: Doubleday, 1956.

Borg, Marcus. *Convictions*. New York: HarperOne, 2014.

Borysenko, Joan. *Minding the Body, Mending the Mind*. Reading, MA: Addison-Wesley, 1987.

Brown, Matthew. *Debussy Redux: The Impact of His Music on Popular Culture.* Bloomington: Indiana University Press, 2012.

Brown, Rosemary. *Unfinished Symphonies: Voices from the Beyond.* New York: Morrow, 1971.

Buckingham, Jamie. *Daughter of Destiny: The Authorized Biography of Kathryn Kuhlman.* Plainfield, NJ: Logos, 1997.

Burleigh, Nina. *A Very Private Woman: The Life and Unsolved Murder of Presidential Mistress Mary Meyer.* New York: Bantam Books, 1998.

Burton, Thomas. *Serpent-Handling Believers.* Knoxville: University of Tennessee Press, 1993.

Byrne, Rhonda. *The Secret.* New York: Simon & Schuster, 2006.

Corinda, Tony. *Thirteen Steps to Mentalism.* New York: Louis Tannen, 1968.

Coué, Emile. *Self Mastery through Conscious Autosuggestion.* New York: American Library, 1922.

Daugherty, Mary Lee. "Serpent-Handling as Sacrament." *Theology Today* 33, no. 3 (October 1976).

Ford, Arthur. *Unknown but Known: My Adventure into the Meditative Dimension.* New York: Harper & Row, 1968.

Ford, Arthur, with Margueritte Harmon Bro. *Nothing So Strange: The Autobiography of Arthur Ford.* New York: Harper & Sons, 1958.

Freeman, Hobart E. *Angels of Light? How to Be Set Free from Occult Oppression and Bondage.* Plainfield, NJ: Logos, 1971.

Gasson, Raphael. *The Challenging Counterfeit: An Exposé of Psychic Phenomena.* Plainfield, NJ: Logos, 1969.

Godwin, John. *Super-Psychic: The Incredible Dr. Hoy.* New York: Pocket Books, 1974.

Graham, Billy. *Peace with God.* New York: Doubleday, 1953.

———. *World Aflame.* New York: Doubleday, 1963.

Gresham, William L. *Nightmare Alley.* New York: Signet, 1946.

Griffiths, R. R., W. A. Richards, U. McCann, and R. Jesse. "Psilocybin Can Occasion Mystical-Type Experiences Having Substantial and Sustained Personal Meaning and Spiritual Significance." *Psychopharmacology* 187 (2006): 268–83.

Hayman, Ronald. *A Life of Jung.* New York: Norton, 1999.

Hill, Napoleon. *Think and Grow Rich*. Meriden, CT: Ralston, 1937.

Hines, Terence. *Pseudoscience and the Paranormal*. Amherst, NY: Prometheus, 2003.

Houdini, Harry. *A Magician among the Spirits*. New York: Harper, 1924.

———. *Miracle Mongers and Their Methods*. New York: Dutton, 1920.

Hunter, Roy. *The Art of Spiritual Hypnosis: Accessing Divine Wisdom*. New York: Blooming Twigg, 2016.

Hutchinson, Roger. *Aleister Crowley: The Beast Demystified*. Edinburgh: Mainstream, 1998.

Jaher, David. *The Witch of Lime Street: Séance, Seduction, and Houdini in the Spirit World*. New York: Crown, 2015.

James, William. *Varieties of Religious Experience*. New York: Penguin, 1985.

Janney, Peter. *Mary's Mosaic: The CIA Conspiracy to Murder John F. Kennedy, Mary Pinchot Meyer, and Their Vision for World Peace*. 3rd ed. New York: Skyhorse Publishing, 2013.

Jastrow, Joseph. *The Psychology of Conviction: A Study of Beliefs and Attitudes*. New York: Houghton Mifflin, 1918.

Kappas, John G. *Professional Hypnotism Manual*. Rev. ed. Tarzana, CA: Panorama, 2001.

———. *Success Is Not an Accident: The Mental Bank Concept*. Tarzana, CA: Panorama, 1987.

Keating, Thomas. *Intimacy with God*. New York: Crossroad, 1994.

———. *Open Mind, Open Heart: The Contemplative Dimension of the Gospel*. New York: Continuum, 2003.

Keene, M. Lamar. *The Psychic Mafia*. New York: St. Martin's, 1976.

Kirkpatrick, Sidney D. *Edgar Cayce: An American Prophet*. New York: Riverhead, 2000.

Koenig, Harold G. *The Healing Power of Faith: Science Explores Medicine's Last Great Frontier*. New York: Simon & Schuster, 2001.

Kole, André, and Al Janssen. *From Illusion to Reality*. San Bernardino, CA: Here's Life, 1984.

Korem, Dan. *The Art of Profiling: Reading People Right the First Time*. Richardson, TX: IFP, 1998.

———. *Psychic Confession*. Dallas: Korem Productions, 1986.

Korem, Dan, and Paul Meier. *The Fakers: Exploding the Myths of the Supernatural.* Rev. ed. Grand Rapids: Baker Books, 1980.

Kübler-Ross, Elisabeth. *On Death & Dying.* New York: Simon & Schuster, 1969.

Lamont, Peter, and Jim Steinmeyer. *The Secret History of Magic.* New York: TarcherPerigee, 2018.

London, Nicole, producer/codirector. *Harriet Tubman: Visions of Freedom.* Video. Owings Mills, MD: Maryland Public Television, 2022.

Malina, Bruce J., and John J. Pilch. *Social Science Commentary on the Book of Acts.* Minneapolis: Fortress, 2008.

Matthews, Dale. *The Faith Factor: Proof of the Healing Power of Prayer.* New York: Penguin, 1998.

Maynard, N. C. *Was Abraham Lincoln a Spiritualist?* Philadelphia: Rufus C. Hartranft, 1891.

McNamara, Patrick. *The Neuroscience of Sleep and Dreams.* 2nd ed. Cambridge: Cambridge University Press, 2023.

Meier, Paul, and Robert Wise. *Windows of the Soul: A Look at Dreams and Their Meanings.* Nashville: Nelson, 1995.

Mongan, Marie. *Hypnobirthing: A Natural Approach to a Safe, Easier, More Comfortable Birthing.* Palm Beach, FL: HCI, 2015.

Murphy, Nancey. *Bodies and Souls, or Spiritual Bodies?* Cambridge: Cambridge University Press, 2006.

Navarro, Joe. *What Every Body Is Saying.* New York: Morrow, 2008.

Nee, Watchman. *The Latent Power of the Soul.* Reprint. Richmond, VA: Christian Fellowship, 1972.

Nestor, James. *Breath: The New Science of a Lost Art.* New York: Penguin, 2020.

Newberg, Andrew. *Neurotheology: How Science Can Enlighten Us about Spirituality.* New York: Columbia University Press, 2021.

Newberg, Andrew, and Mark Robert Waldman. *How God Changes Your Brain: Breakthrough Findings from a Leading Neuroscientist.* New York: Ballantine, 2010.

Orloff, Judith. *Intuitive Healing.* New York: Random House, 2000.

Peale, Norman Vincent. *The Power of Positive Thinking.* New York: Prentice-Hall, 1952.

Pert, Candace B. *Molecules of Emotion: Why You Feel the Way You Feel*. New York: Scribner's Sons, 1997.

Pike, James, with Diane Kennedy. *The Other Side: An Account of My Experiences with Psychic Phenomena*. Garden City, NY: Doubleday, 1968.

Pike, Kenneth L. *Language in Relation to a Unified Theory of the Structure of Human Behavior*. 2nd rev. ed. The Hague: Moulton, 1967.

———. *Talk, Thought, and Thing: The Emic Road toward Conscious Knowledge*. Dallas: Summer Institute of Linguistics, 1993.

Randi, James. "The Project Alpha Experiment Part One." *Skeptical Inquirer* 7, no. 4 (Summer 1983).

———. "The Project Alpha Experiment Part Two." *Skeptical Inquirer* 8, no. 1 (Fall 1993).

———. *The Truth about Uri Geller*. Amherst, NY: Prometheus, 1982.

Rapaport, Brooke Kamin. *Houdini: Art and Magic*. New Haven: Yale University Press, 2010.

Rauscher, William V. *The Houdini Code Mystery: A Spirit Secret Solved*. Pasadena, CA: Magic Words, 2000.

———. *Religion, Magic, and the Supernatural*. Woodbury, NJ: Mystic Light, 2006.

———. *The Spiritual Frontier*. New York: Doubleday, 1975.

Rosen, Sidney. *My Voice Will Go with You: The Teaching Tales of Milton H. Ericson*. New York: Norton, 1991.

Rossi, Ernest L., and Daniel B. Cheek. *Mind-Body Therapy: Methods of Ideodynamic Healing in Hypnosis*. New York: Norton, 1988.

Rowland, Ian. *The Full Facts Book of Cold Reading*. London: Ian Rowland, 1998.

Schuller, Robert H. *Move Ahead with Possibility Thinking*. New York: Doubleday, 1967.

Schulz, Mona Lisa. *Awakening Intuition: Using Your Mind-Body Network for Insight and Healing*. New York: Harmony, 1998.

Schwartz, Berthold E. "Taming the Poltergeist (Clinical Observations on Steve Shaw's Telekinesis)." *Journal of the American Society of Psychosomatic Dentistry and Medicine* 29, no. 4, supplement 6 (1982).

Schwartz, Scott. *Faith, Serpents, and Fire: Images of Kentucky Holiness Believers*. Jackson: University of Mississippi Press, 1999.

Scot, Reginald. *The Discoverie of Witchcraft.* New York: Dover, 1972.

Siegel, Bernie S. *Love, Medicine, and Miracles.* New York: Harper & Row, 1988.

Spiegel, Herbert, and David Spiegel. *Trance and Treatment: Clinical Uses of Hypnosis.* New York: Basic Books, 1978.

Spraggett, Allen, with William V. Rauscher. *Arthur Ford: The Man Who Talked with the Dead.* New York: New American Library, 1973.

Steiger, Brad. *In My Soul I Am Free.* Crystal, MN: Illuminated Way, 1968.

Stevenson, Ian. *Twenty Cases of Reincarnation.* Charlottesville: University of Virginia Press, 1966.

Streett, R. Alan. *Caesar and the Sacrament: Baptism; A Rite of Resistance.* Eugene, OR: Cascade, 2018.

———. *The Effective Invitation: A Practical Guide for the Pastor.* Old Tappan, NJ: Revell, 1984; reprint, Grand Rapids: Kregel, 1995. Rev. and updated, 2004.

———. *Heaven on Earth: Experiencing the Kingdom of God in the Here and Now.* Eugene, OR: Harvest House, 2013.

———. *In High Places: A Study of Occult and Government.* Finksburg, MD: SMI, 1977.

———. "An Interview with Gary Elkins." *Criswell Theological Review* 7, no. 2 (Spring 2010).

———. *The Invaders: A Biblical Study of UFO's.* Finksburg, MD: SMI, 1975.

———. *The Occult: Its Demonic Nature.* Finksburg, MD: SMI, 1975.

———. "Snake Handling and Mark 16:18 — Primitive Christianity or Indigenous American Religion." *Criswell Theological Review* 8, no. 1 (Fall 2010).

———. *Songs of Resistance: Challenging Caesar and Empire.* Eugene, OR: Cascade, 2022.

———. *Subversive Meals: An Analysis of the Lord's Supper under Roman Domination during the First Century.* Eugene, OR: Pickwick, 2013.

Sugrue, Thomas. *There Is a River: The Story of Edgar Cayce.* New York: Dell, 1967.

Tarbell, Harlan. *Tarbell Course in Magic.* Vol. 1. Brooklyn, NY: D. Robbins, 1971.

Unger, Merrill F. *The Haunting of Bishop Pike: A Christian View of the Other Side*. Wheaton, IL: Tyndale House, 1971.

Weisberg, Barbara. *Talking to the Dead: Kate and Maggie Fox and the Rise of Spiritualism*. New York: HarperCollins, 2004.

Wicker, Christine. *Lily Dale: The True Story of the Town That Talks to the Dead*. New York: HarperCollins, 2003.

Wilkerson, David, with John Sherrill and Elizabeth Sherrill. *The Cross and the Switchblade*. New York: Bernard Geis Associates, 1963.

Worrall, Ambrose, and Olga Worrall. *Explore Your Psychic World*. New York: Harper & Row, 1970.

——. *The Gift of Healing*. New York: Harper & Row, 1965.

Yaden, David B. *The Varieties of Spiritual Experience: 21st Century Research and Perspectives*. Oxford: Oxford University Press, 2022.

Yogananda, Paramhansa. *Autobiography of a Yogi*. New York: Philosophical Library, 1946.

Index